NON-LETHAL WEAPONS

Too often, military and law enforcement authorities have found themselves constrained by inadequate weaponry: the tools available to them, in addressing confrontations with entrenched opponents of various sorts, are either too weak (not sufficing to disarm or defeat the enemy) or too strong (generating unacceptable "collateral damage" in harming innocent people or property). An emerging category of "non-lethal weapons" carries promise for resolving this dilemma, proffering new capabilities for disabling opponents without inflicting death or permanent injury. This array of sophisticated technologies is being rapidly developed and could emerge for use by soldiers and police in the near future. These augmented capabilities carry both immense promise and grave risks: they expand the power of law enforcement and military units, enabling them to accomplish assigned missions with greater finesse and fewer casualties. But they may also be misused – increasing malign applications and inspiring leaders to overrely on a myth of "bloodless combat." This book explores the emerging world of non-lethal weapons by examining a series of case studies – recent real-world scenarios from five confrontations around the world in which the availability of a modern arsenal might have made a difference.

David A. Koplow is a professor of law at the Georgetown University Law Center and director of a clinic, the Center for Applied Legal Studies, in which students represent refugees who seek political asylum in the United States because of persecution on account of race, religion, or political opinion in their homelands. After graduating from Yale Law School in 1978, Koplow served the U.S. government in the Arms Control and Disarmament Agency (1978–81 as Attorney-Adviser and as Special Assistant to the Director) and in the Department of Defense (1997–9 as Deputy General Counsel for International Affairs). In the latter capacity, he was the senior legal specialist for the top Pentagon leadership on the full array of international legal issues, including use of military force in the Persian Gulf and Kosovo, negotiation and implementation of treaties, the law of the sea, programs of military cooperation and assistance, and the law of outer space. He has published many articles dealing with treaties and U.S. constitutional law in law journals and has published books on national security and arms control policy.

NON-LETHAL WEAPONS

THE LAW AND POLICY OF REVOLUTIONARY
TECHNOLOGIES FOR THE MILITARY
AND LAW ENFORCEMENT

DAVID A. KOPLOW

Georgetown University Law Center

CAMBRIDGE
UNIVERSITY PRESS

CAMBRIDGE UNIVERSITY PRESS
Cambridge, New York, Melbourne, Madrid, Cape Town, Singapore, São Paulo

Cambridge University Press
40 West 20th Street, New York, NY 10011-4211, USA

www.cambridge.org
Information on this title: www.cambridge.org/9780521857581

First published 2006

Printed in the United States of America

A catalog record for this publication is available from the British Library.

Library of Congress Cataloging in Publication Data

Koplow, David A., 1951–
Non-lethal weapons : the law and policy for the military and law
enforcement / David A. Koplow. – 1st ed.
p. cm.
Includes bibliographical references and index.
ISBN-13: 978-0-521-85758-1 (hardback : alk. paper)
ISBN-10: 0-521-85758-9 (hardback : alk. paper)
ISBN-13: 978-0-521-67435-5 (pbk. : alk. paper)
ISBN-10: 0-521-67435-2 (pbk. : alk. paper)
1. Nonlethal weapons.   I. Title.
K3661.K67 2006
363.2′32–dc22   2005028816

ISBN-13 978-0-521-85758-1 hardback
ISBN-10 0-521-85758-9 hardback

ISBN-13 978-0-521-67435-5 paperback
ISBN-10 0-521-67435-2 paperback

To my Mother

Contents

Acknowledgments

The author expresses deepest gratitude to the following people who provided invaluable insights for my research, reviewed earlier drafts of the manuscript, and assisted in numerous other ways: Karen Blum, James Burger, Robin Coupland, George Fenton, David Fidler, Charles S. "Sid" Heal, Joseph A. Rutigliano Jr., and Malcolm Wiener.

The author also thanks his talented and diligent research assistants: Matthew Dubeck, Frederick Lohr, Patrick Moulding, and Andrea Truelove.

An earlier version of the analysis contained in this book was published in Volume 36 of the *Georgetown Journal of International Law* as "Tangled Up in Khaki and Blue: Lethal and Non-Lethal Weapons in Recent Confrontations."

ONE

Introduction

The governmental mechanisms that exercise a state's physical coercive power – various cadres of military and law enforcement agencies – often face a difficult dilemma. In confrontations with recalcitrant opposing forces of varying sorts, the authorities must recognize that if they exercise *too much* power, they incur an unacceptable danger of "collateral damage" – unintended casualties to civilians and unnecessary destruction of valuable property. On the other hand, if they exercise *too little* power, they may risk the safety of their own personnel and compromise the accomplishment of an important and legitimate mission.

In recent years, this dilemma has arisen with painful frequency inside the United States and elsewhere, and officials increasingly express frustration at having only an impoverished array of tools at their disposal, especially regarding confrontations in which the specific target of the police or military forces is intermingled with civilians or innocent bystanders. Government actors may have only "bullhorns or bullets" to choose from – if emphatic verbal instructions and warnings do not suffice, the only recourse is to the application of deadly force, which often cannot be applied with anything like the desired surgical precision.

This book examines that dilemma in the context of the imminent development of a novel toolkit of so-called non-lethal weapons

(NLWs), which promise radically to alter the existing Hobson's choice. These armaments – a wide range of technologies, new and old, incorporating different types of physical mechanisms, capable of both antipersonnel and antimateriel operations – seek to provide a viable intermediate capability, for the first time affording governmental actors additional options in these volatile situations. These emerging resources include a breathtaking array of devices such as enhancements of the traditional "rubber bullets," foam sprays that make a surface either impossibly slippery or impassively sticky, millimeter-wave "heat rays" that peacefully repel people without inflicting lasting harm, projectile netting or other entangling devices to capture individuals or vehicles, chemicals that temporarily irritate, repel, or becalm a person, biological agents that embrittle metal or contaminate petroleum products, and much more.

The methodology of the book is to examine five representative recent confrontations – the 1993 shootout and siege at Waco, Texas, involving federal ATF and FBI units against the Branch Davidians led by millennialist David Koresh; the 1994 genocide in Rwanda, in which the United Nations, the United States, France, and other outside forces were so shamefully passive; the 1996–7 terrorist takeover of the Japanese ambassador's residence in Lima, Peru; the 2002 seizure of the Dubrovka Theater in Moscow by Chechen separatists; and the 2003 Gulf War II fighting by the British Army against indigenous resistance in Basra, Iraq. Although in each of these episodes the government forces "prevailed," in some crude sense, each was at least partially unsatisfactory – they resulted in more carnage and more destruction than anyone would have wanted. So the goal is to determine whether the availability of a richer configuration of NLWs might have made a difference.

These five case studies provide an array of contrasts: they occurred on five different continents, they involved five different countries and five different types of resistance units as protagonists, and they engaged notably different genres of armaments and tactics. In addition, the selected incidents are usefully diverse in yet another regard. Some (Waco and Lima) were clearly law enforcement operations – in the Texas example, initially occasioned by the effort to serve ordinary arrest and search warrants. In contrast, the fifth case (Basra) was plainly a conventional military operation, occurring in the midst of a broad-gauged international armed conflict. The Moscow incident presents a sort of middle ground, containing aspects of both law enforcement and military counterterrorism operations, thereby illuminating the rainbow of legal and policy considerations at play. Rwanda is similarly difficult to categorize, as it incorporates elements of coup d'état, civil war, and genocide.

The book does not argue that non-lethal weapons *should* have been applied in all these confrontations, or that they necessarily *would* have made a profound difference in resolving the clashes at appreciably less cost. It may be that these instances were simply intractable, that the opposing forces were so resistant, fanatic, or entrenched that even improved technology and tactics would have proven unavailing. Still, the hypothetical inquiry remains: what might have happened, in these five tragic cases, if the respective governments had been able to try something else – something non-lethal?

The book proceeds in the following steps. First, the emerging world of NLWs is surveyed, beginning with the observation that the very name "non-lethal" is at least partially misleading: any application of force by police or military units inherently carries the potential for death. Although this new family of technologies attempts at least to reduce greatly the probability of mortality and widespread destruction of property, there can be no absolute guaranties.

Chapter 2 also describes a variety of NLW technologies, starting with the more familiar devices (tear gas, water cannon, plastic bullets, etc.) long used by governments around the world. It then introduces some of the more tantalizing possibilities that loom on, or just over, the horizon: gizmos that disable or deter, ensnare or blockade, corrode or contaminate, all without inflicting catastrophic harm. The chapter also describes some of the animating spirit behind the investigation of, and the burgeoning investment in, these esoteric capabilities: the classic scenarios in which military and police forces imagine they would be better able to control incendiary situations, perform their assigned missions, and protect themselves and any bystanders with greatly reduced fatalities and destruction.

Chapter 3 next assesses the law applicable to NLWs, starting with the international legal constraints upon battlefield violence. Treaties that regulate chemical, biological, and other categories of specialized conventional armaments are highlighted, along with the more general evolving law of armed conflict, which was crafted largely with other kinds of implements of war in mind, but which must now adapt to embrace NLWs as well. Domestic U.S. law, too, governs non-lethals, constraining both the research on selected armaments concepts and the application of force by federal and local law enforcement in contentious situations. In particular, the prohibition against, and the definition of, "excessive" force by police demands attention in the context of NLW?

Next, the five selected case studies are presented: Waco (Chapter 4), Rwanda (Chapter 5), Lima (Chapter 6), Moscow (Chapter 7), and Basra (Chapter 8). Recent events have provided an altogether-too-rich assortment of unhappy incidents of collective violence to choose from, but these five representatives may usefully characterize the field. Each of these five confrontations has already been described in the relevant literature, so the focus here is not to retell each story in lurid detail, but to concentrate on the types of weapons used by police, military, and their opponents. More tellingly, the inquiry asks about the types of weapons that were *not* used in each incident: what might have happened, how might things have turned out differently, if an additional category of weapons, with a variety of specialized non-lethal effects and attributes, had been available?

The point here is not simply to critique the beleaguered combatants or to second-guess their choices of negotiating strategies, political positions, or assault tactics. Instead, the book poses the hypothetical inquiry about whether NLWs could have played a useful contributing role in saving lives, protecting property, and accomplishing missions.

Chapter 9 then sounds a necessary cautionary note, recording some of the many critiques of the nascent movement to embrace NLWs, and exploring a miscellany of arguments why we might still hesitate to go wholeheartedly down this procurement pathway. Even if one believes that NLWs could have made a positive contribution to a more-peaceful resolution of the five selected case studies, there are counterbalancing considerations to consider. Prominent among these concerns are the danger of proliferation of the weaponry (to opposing military forces, criminals, or human rights abusers) and the release of existing inhibitions against too-adventurous applications of governmental force.

Finally, Chapter 10 offers some recommendations and conclusions, boiling down to a cautious "green light" for NLW development programs. There are good reasons to be hopeful that emerging non-lethal technologies can liberate police and military forces from their existing dilemma: if you have only the ability to overreact or to underreact, you can't do a very good job of promoting law, order, and security. If sticky foam, acoustic rays, tasers, vehicle nets, and other esoteric devices could enable military and law enforcement authorities to behave with a more deft touch, complementing existing firepower with an enriched range of possibilities, that would be a most welcome boon. But international and domestic law restraints, and the prudent projections about how other actors might respond to our articulation of new NLW capabilities, mandate a reflective, step-by-step approach. NLWs might be helpful, indeed, in some categories of important, challenging, and all-too-frequent confrontations, but they are no panacea.

TWO

The World of Non-Lethal Weapons

A. DEFINING "NON-LETHAL"

What do we mean by "non-lethal" weapons? A variety of definitions has been proffered, the most visible of which comes from the U.S. Department of Defense, where the U.S. Marine Corps houses the Joint Non-Lethal Weapons Directorate (JNLWD), the leading military arm in interservice research, development, and procurement in the field. As specified in the definition section of DoD Directive 3000.3,

3.1. Non-Lethal Weapons. Weapons that are explicitly designed and primarily employed so as to incapacitate personnel or materiel, while minimizing fatalities, permanent injury to personnel, and undesired damage to property and the environment.

3.1.1. Unlike conventional lethal weapons that destroy their targets principally through blast, penetration and fragmentation, non-lethal weapons employ means other than gross physical destruction to prevent the target from functioning.

3.1.2. Non-lethal weapons are intended to have one, or both, of the following characteristics:

3.1.2.1. They have relatively reversible effects on personnel or materiel.

3.1.2.2. They affect objects differently within their area of influence.[1]

---

[1] Department of Defense Directive No. 3000.3, Policy for Non-Lethal Weapons, July 9, 1996.

In partial contrast, the National Institute of Justice, which orchestrates the U.S. Department of Justice's exploratory programs in the law enforcement side of the NLW field, articulates the objective as the "identification and development of new or improved weapons and other technology that will minimize the risk of death and injury to officers, suspects, prisoners and the public, and contribute to the reduction of civil and criminal liability suits against police, sheriff, and corrections departments."[2]

Other experts have promulgated rival definitions, with varying degrees of formality and inclusiveness.[3] NATO, for example, formally refers to the area as encompassing "weapons which are explicitly designed and developed to incapacitate or repel personnel, with a low probability of fatality or permanent injury, or to disable equipment with minimal undesired damage or impact on the environment."[4]

For purposes of this book, it is useful to supplement these working definitions, by differentiating more precisely between antipersonnel and antimateriel NLWs, along the following lines: antipersonnel NLWs are weapons designed and used to have relatively temporary effects, which disappear either simply via the passage of time or via the administration of relatively minor treatment. Antimateriel NLWs are weapons that are designed and used either (a) to have relatively temporary effects, which disappear either simply via the passage of time or via the administration of relatively minor

---

[2] National Institute of Justice, quoted in Lois Pilant, Crime and War: An Analysis of Non-Lethal Technologies and Weapons Development, 65 *The Police Chief* No. 6, June 1998, p. 55.

[3] The Human Effects Advisory Panel established by the JNLWD has proposed a quantitative definition, under which a weapon would be classified as non-lethal if it incapacitates 98 percent of the people it is used against, while killing no more than 1/2 percent, permanently injuring no more than 1/2 percent, and having no effect on 1 percent. Cited in David P. Fidler, The International Legal Implications of "Non-Lethal" Weapons, 21 *Michigan Journal of International Law* 51, fall 1999, p. 62 (hereinafter Fidler Michigan).

[4] NATO Policy on Non-Lethal Weapons, Press Statement, October 13, 1999.

treatment, or (b) to damage or destroy a target via nonexplosive means.[5] It is important to note that none of these definitions includes any complete assurance against lethal effects of the weaponry. The effort is to *reduce* the probability of mortality, but not necessarily to negate it altogether; in any application of organized violence, especially one undertaken in such a wide variety of environments and contexts, against people of diverse health histories, strengths, and weaknesses, there is some inherent, irreducible danger of fatalities. A projectile, chemical, or other mechanism that would merely disable or temporarily incapacitate one person (e.g., a young, healthy soldier in the open air) might well inflict mortal injury on someone else (e.g., a child in a confined space or an elderly person already compromised by illness).[6]

Many observers, therefore, regarding the very term "non-lethal weapon" as an oxymoron, have substituted alternative vocabularies. They would refer to the topic as embracing weapons that are "sublethal," "less lethal," "less than lethal," "disabling" or that

[5] As elaborated infra, these definitions bring within the embrace of NLWs weapons that are either (a) temporary (in allowing the targeted person or object to return to ordinary functioning relatively quickly) or (b) stealthy (in permanently destroying an object via mechanisms that are relatively unusual, precise, and quiet). For present purposes, we dispense with potential NLWs (e.g., specialized chemical or biological weapons) that might be designed specifically to target plants or animals.

This book follows the literature's convention in excluding from the current discussion consideration of a variety of other weapons, tactics, and programs that typically would be "non-lethal," at least in their initial effects, but that raise so many sui generis issues of their own that separate analysis is warranted. Among these most important topics – related to, but different from, the NLWs described here – are computer warfare, psychological operations, robotics, nanotechnology, precision guidance, and advanced sensor systems.

[6] Realistically, the opposite pole of the spectrum of lethality is also merely a matter of probability: even the most "lethal" of traditional weapons are fatal in only a fraction of their applications. Battlefield statistics indicate that Kalashnikov rifles, for example, kill only 20 percent of the soldiers they injure, and hand grenade injuries are fatal only 10 percent of the time. Robin M. Coupland and David Meddings, Mortality Associated with Use of Weapons in Armed Conflicts, Wartime Atrocities, and Civilian Mass Shootings: Literature Review, 319 *British Medical Journal* 407, August 14, 1999.

accomplish a "soft kill" or a "mission kill." For similar reasons, the International Committee of the Red Cross and some other authors, when referring to this entire category of ordnance, routinely place the term "non-lethal weapons" inside quotation marks, or use a phrase like "so-called non-lethal weapons."[7]

While acknowledging the somewhat misleading connotation of the term, this book will follow the mainstream of the literature and employ the term "non-lethal" (ordinarily without quotation marks). For better or worse, this is the language that has established itself as the leading expression, and, lacking an obviously better alternative, it remains a plausible form of reference.

B. TRADITIONAL FORMS OF NON-LETHAL WEAPONS

The concept of a NLW is hardly a recent creation. Indeed, a variety of NLWs has been a staple in the inventories of armies – and especially of police – around the world for decades. Among the most familiar low-technology devices for crowd control have been truncheons, water cannon, K-9 corps, and cattle prods. One step higher on the ladder of escalation have been rubber or plastic bullets – or, more generally, firearms that utilize projectiles (including aerodynamic beanbags, wooden batons, and composite plugs) that inflict a blunt trauma upon the target, without intending to penetrate the skin or

---

[7] See, e.g., Robin M. Coupland, "Calmatives" and "Incapacitants": Questions for International Humanitarian Law Brought by New Means and Methods of Warfare with New Effects?, 19th Workshop of the Pugwash Study Group on the Implementation of the Chemical and Biological Weapons Conventions, April 26–7, 2003 (hereinafter Coupland Calmatives); Fidler Michigan, supra note 3, at 60 (asserting that "the term 'non-lethal' persists not because more accurate terms cannot be found but because it is easier for the military to market 'non-lethal' weapons in military and civilian contexts"). The Department of Justice traditionally has referred to this topic as the investigation of "less than lethal" systems, whereas the Department of Defense has adopted "non-lethal."

inflict fatal wounds. A different approach comes from the world of chemistry: law enforcement officials in the United States, the United Kingdom, and many other countries have employed sequential generations of tear gas or other noxious vapors, especially those designated CN (including the Mace brand) or CS.

These devices and tactics proliferated across the country and around the world – and they frequently recorded at least partial, tactical successes. In many instances, police use of these limited, albeit crude, measures aided in breaking up a crowd, isolating the most determined opponents, and deterring the more faint of heart. In several turbulent settings, authorities succeeded in protecting property, fracturing an illegal demonstration, apprehending the ringleaders, and avoiding further inciting the populace.

But these immature mechanisms were burdened with important defects and limitations. Many operated only at short range – for example, a police officer would have to come within arm's length of the offender to strike with a nightstick – and that proximity could be hazardous in situations where the police might be outnumbered. Some of the devices were unreliable (the electric charge in a cattle prod might fail, or might be insufficient to alter the target's behavior) or subject to available countermeasures (crowds could avoid water cannon, or outmaneuver or outlast the vehicles transporting it). Chemical sprays could be dissipated by adverse weather – rain would degrade some chemicals very quickly – and a capricious wind could turn the gas back onto the police themselves. Importantly, these devices were sometimes far more than non-lethal; deaths from plastic bullets, for example, were not uncommon, as a projectile might strike a particularly vulnerable person, might hit someone at a closer range than anticipated, or might impact a sensitive body part. And, of course, the public reaction to these displays of force was frequently adverse – police sometimes seemed to create additional enemies, and damage their own reputations, even when they were sincerely attempting to modulate their application of restrained power.

C. MODERN NON-LETHAL WEAPON CONCEPTS

The turn of the century is ushering in a dramatically new era of NLWs; a bewildering array of unforeseen capabilities is now set to spill out of laboratories and test sites. The literature on NLWs has likewise mushroomed, including contributions from public policy,[8] medicine,[9] popular culture,[10] military science,[11] and law.[12]

[8] The Council on Foreign Relations has sponsored a series of three independent task forces to analyze NLWs and make recommendations for future actions. Council on Foreign Relations, Independent Task Force (Malcolm Wiener, chair), Non-Lethal Technologies: Military Options and Implications (1995); Council on Foreign Relations, Independent Task Force (Richard Garwin, chair), Nonlethal Technologies: Progress and Prospects (1999) (hereinafter CFR 2); and Council on Foreign Relations, Independent Task Force (Graham Allison and Paul X. Kelley, cochairs), Nonlethal Weapons and Capabilities (2004) (hereinafter CFR 3). The author was a member of the third task force. Other public policy organizations such as the Sunshine Project and the Federation of American Scientists have focused attention on selected NLW options, bringing to public attention a variety of important documents and analyses. See www.sunshine-project.org and www.fas.org/man/dod-101/sys/land/non-lethal.htm.

[9] See, e.g., Jean-Paul Yih, CS Gas Injury to the Eye, 311 British Medical Journal No. 7000, July 29, 1995, p. 276; "Safety" of Chemical Batons, 352 Lancet No. 9123, July 18, 1998, p. 159; James S. Ketchum and Frederick R. Sidell, Incapacitating Agents, in Frederick R. Sidell et al. (eds.), Medical Aspects of Chemical and Biological Warfare, Office of the Surgeon General, U.S. Army (1997), pp. 287–306.

[10] Eric Adams, Shoot to Not Kill, 262 Popular Science No. 5, May 2003, p. 88; John Barry and Tom Morganthau, Soon, "Phasers on Stun," Newsweek, February 7, 1994, p. 24; Stephen Mihm, The Quest for the Nonkiller App, New York Times Magazine, July 25, 2004, p. 38.

[11] U.S. Army Center for Army Lessons Learned, Civil Disturbances: Incorporating Non-Lethal Technology: Tactics, Techniques and Procedures, Newsletter 00–7, April 2000; Robert T. Durkin, The Operational Use of Non-Lethal Weapons, Naval War College, February 8, 2000; Timothy J. Lamb, Emerging Nonlethal Weapons Technology and Strategic Policy Implications for 21st Century Warfare, thesis, U.S. Army War College, Carlisle Barracks, Penn., 1998; Robert Mandel, Nonlethal Weaponry and Post–Cold War Deterrence, 30 Armed Forces & Society No. 4, summer 2004, p. 511.

[12] Neal Miller, Less-than-Lethal Force Weaponry: Law Enforcement and Correctional Agency Civil Law Liability for the Use of Excessive Force, 28 Creighton Law Review No. 3, April 1995, pp. 733–94; James C. Duncan, A Primer on the Employment of Non-Lethal Weapons, 45 Naval Law Review, 1998, pp. 1–55; Fidler Michigan, supra

C. MODERN NON-LETHAL WEAPON CONCEPTS

Both U.S.[13] and international[14] authorities (especially British)[15] are engaged, and a variety of academic and commercial NLW activities have captured the imagination.[16] The U.S. government has started to devote significant funds to the area,[17] and our NATO allies are being brought to the topic, as well – despite criticisms that progress has not been as rapid as promised.[18]

note 3; Vincent Sautenet, Legal Issues Concerning Military Use of Non-Lethal Weapons, 7 *Murdoch University Electronic Journal of Law* No. 2, June 2000.

[13] See, e.g., Lynn Klotz, Martin Furmanski, and Mark Wheelis, Beware the Siren's Song: Why "Non-Lethal" Incapacitating Chemical Agents Are Lethal, Federation of American Scientists, March 2003; Mark Wheelis, "Nonlethal" Chemical Weapons: A Faustian Bargain, 19 *Issues in Science and Technology* No. 3, spring 2003, p. 74.

[14] See, e.g., Coupland Calmatives, supra note 7; Isabelle Daoust, Robin Coupland, and Rikke Ishoey, New Wars, New Weapons? The Obligation of States to Assess the Legality of Means and Methods of Warfare, 84 *International Review of the Red Cross* No. 846, June 2002, p. 345; Friedhelm Kruger-Sprengel, Non-Lethal Weapons: A Humanitarian Perspective in Modern Conflict, 42 *The Military Law and the Law of War Review* Nos. 3–4, 2003, p. 359.

[15] Malcolm R. Dando, The Danger to the Chemical Weapons Convention from Incapacitating Chemicals, Strengthening the Chemical Weapons Convention, First CWC Review Conference Paper No. 4, March 2003; Nick Lewer and Steven Schofield, *Non-Lethal Weapons: A Fatal Attraction? Military Strategies and Technologies for 21st Century Conflict* (1997); and a series of research reports from the Centre for Conflict Resolution, Non-Lethal Weapons Research Project at Bradford University (U.K.): Nick Lewer, Introduction to Non-Lethal Weapons, Research Report Number 1 (November 1997); Nick Lewer, Research Report Number 2 (June 1998); Tobias Feakin, Research Report Number 3 (August 2001); Neil Davison and Nick Lewer, Research Report Number 4 (December 2003); Neil Davison and Nick Lewer, Research Report Number 5 (May 2004); Neil Davison and Nick Lewer, Research Report Number 6 (October 2004); Neil Davidson and Nick Lewer, Research Report Number 7 (May 2005).

[16] On academic activities, see, e.g., Non-Lethal Technology Innovation Center, University of New Hampshire, www.unh.edu/ntic; Nonlethal Environmental Evaluation and Remediation Center, Kansas State University, www.engg.ksu.edu/NEER/nonlethal; Institute for Non-Lethal Defense Technology, Pennsylvania State University, www.arl.psu.edu/core/nonlethal. On commercial activities, see Malcolm Dando (ed.), Non-Lethal Weapons: Technological and Operational Prospects, Jane's online special report (November 2000), Introduction (noting four international conferences on NLWs sponsored by Jane's Information Group starting in 1997).

[17] Because many NLW development programs are classified, it is impossible to track the U.S. government's entire annual spending on NLWs. One crude, partial indicator is the budget of the JNLWD, which oversees certain multiservice research and development programs. This account has grown from $9.3 million in FY 1997 to $28.1 million in FY 2001 to $43.4 million in FY 2004, with a projection of $45.7 million in FY 2009. CFR 3, supra note 8, at 16. See also CFR 2, supra note 8, at 28–9.

[18] See, e.g., CFR 3, supra note 8, at 8 ("We found little evidence that the value and transformational applications of nonlethal weapons across the spectrum of conflict are appreciated by the senior leadership of the Department of Defense. Despite successes on the small scale, NLW have not entered the mainstream of defense thinking and

Some of the new NLW advances are sequential improvements on existing concepts, incrementally upgrading the current arsenal. Others augur entirely new technologies, never before seen on the battlefield or the streets. A few have already been tried and found wanting – insurmountable (at least for now) technical problems make them infeasible or unattractive. Many are still in development and may similarly fail to meet the complete set of design criteria and operational desiderata. Others, however, have already been deployed to troops in the field or held in reserve for emergencies.[19] This chapter cannot undertake to survey all the NLW technologies in various stages of development. But it can introduce at least a sampling of the most salient, describing a few of the emerging systems, ranging from the increasingly familiar to the "Gee wiz."

Sticky Foam and *Slippery Foam.* Among the earliest modern NLW concepts that fleetingly grabbed public attention in the 1990s were polymer sticky foam and slippery foam. The former would be expelled, like a high-pressure aerosol, from a backpack tank worn by a soldier or police officer. It might reach a range of ten yards or so and douse a targeted person with a moist spray, which would quickly harden to a styrofoam-like rigidity. Once so ensnared, the target could not run away, could not maintain aggressive actions, and could not effectively resist police arrest. Related

procurement"). In the words of U.S. Marine General John Sheehan, NLWs "will always be tomorrow's weapons unless we move now. We need to pull them from the laboratories and place them in operational units." Quoted in Duncan, supra note 12, at 55.

[19] The most advanced example of new operational military non-lethal arms is the creation and distribution of approximately eighty "nonlethal capability sets," which comprise fifty-five types of NLWs in four different modules, including pepper spray, beanbag rounds, plastic handcuffs, spotlights, and shields. JNLWD distributed these sets to U.S. military units around the world, and they were used to good effect in Iraq in 2003, by U.S. Army Quick Reaction Forces that supported small units that found themselves surrounded by hostile crowds. CFR 3, supra note 8, at 13, 18, 28, 49; David P. Karcher, Joint Non-Lethal Weapons Program, January 2003 (slide program).

rigid foam concoctions could be employed to seal a building or vehicle, quickly creating a temporary barrier against entry/egress or movement. Slippery foam would be similarly sprayed from a tank or ejected from a projectile. It would be designed to spread itself to cover a flat surface – a hallway, road, bridge, or runway, for example – with a super-slippery sheen, preventing people from walking or vehicles from driving on it. The prototypes of this "liquid ball bearings" were hundreds of times more slippery than the slickest ice sheets, inspiring the hope that the system could be used, for example, to protect an embassy from an advancing crowd, foreclose enemy use of a strategic intersection or railyard without permanently destroying it, or prevent demonstrators from crossing a coated municipal square.

Unfortunately, the promise to date has exceeded the reality here. Sticky foam (which largely has been abandoned by researchers at least for antipersonnel applications) lost favor because it was not reliably non-lethal; the substance could cover the target's nose and mouth, blocking airways. It also proved laborious to clean up after use.[20] Slippery foam (which is still being actively investigated) might be negated by simple countermeasures – throwing sand or dirt onto the coated surface might quickly and cheaply restore the attackers' traction.

[20] John B. Alexander, *Future War: Non-Lethal Weapons in 21st Century Warfare* (1999), pp. 70–1 (noting that in addition to being potentially lethal, sticky foam is difficult to clean up and requires a bulky recharging unit; nonetheless, it may still prove useful for creating barriers around threatened buildings, even if not for direct antipersonnel use); David G. Boyd, The Search for Low Hanging Fruit: Recent Developments in Non-Lethal Technologies, in Dando, supra note 16, ch. 5 (sticky foam required such painstaking cleanup that it was impractical for law enforcement purposes); Margaret-Anne Coppernoll, The Nonlethal Weapons Debate, 52 *Naval War College Review* 112, spring 1998, p. 5 (noting that freon, which constitutes nearly one-third of sticky foam, is on the list of controlled substances under international and domestic U.S. environmental law because of ozone depletion and is being phased out).

Electric Guns. Instead of a traditional firearm shooting lethal (or sometimes-lethal) projectiles, electricity might be marshaled to stop an attacker, and electromuscular incapacitation devices of various sorts have been developed since the 1970s. Most recently, electric handguns such as the Taser brands M26 and X26 have become quite popular with law enforcement authorities in the United States, the United Kingdom, Canada, and elsewhere. Portable and easy to use, some 135,000 units have been marketed, at prices ranging from $400 to $1,000, with over 200,000 operational or test uses of the devices.

These sidearms (resembling a pistol, but somewhat smaller and lighter) typically eject a pair of small darts, trailing very thin insulated wires, to a distance of twenty-one feet (a longer-range version, to allow engagements at greater standoff distance, is under development). Fishhook-like barbs on the darts attach to the target's skin or clothing, and a brief but powerful electric shock is administered. The electric charge (fifty thousand volts) overrides the subject's central nervous system, causing immediate intense pain, muscle contraction, and loss of muscle control; the subject falls down and becomes unable to resist for five seconds or more.

Proponents assert that the charge is highly effective, even against the most determined (or substance-abusing) resisters, yet no permanent injury is inflicted. In fact, the manufacturer claims hundreds of cases of lives saved when police used tasers instead of handguns to apprehend a dangerous individual. Electric guns are also much more useable in confined spaces, such as inside an aircraft in flight, where use of a conventional bullet would be inadvisable. Over seven thousand police and corrections agencies across the country and elsewhere have adopted this technology, as have many private citizens concerned with personal self-defense. Over two hundred local police departments have purchased tasers for every patrol officer. Recently the U.S. military has placed substantial taser orders, anticipating deployment in Iraq and elsewhere.[21] Critics, on the other hand, challenge the effectiveness and the safety of the system, noting severe or lasting injuries and over one hundred deaths following exposure to taser power. A robust debate has emerged regarding the adequacy of human effects testing conducted to date, with Amnesty International, among others, calling for a moratorium on taser sales, deployments, and use until comprehensive independent health evaluation is undertaken and reliable standards are developed for training and employment of the devices. Recently some local police agencies have backed away from their earlier tentative acceptance of electroshock weaponry.

Opponents also assert that police armed with electric guns are becoming too "quick on the trigger," inappropriately resorting to taser power against unresisting targets when a more restrained, patient approach would suffice. There have also been incidents of tasers proliferating to street criminals, enabling a new genre of "non-lethal crime," and reports of exported electronic weaponry being used for illegitimate interrogation and torture in several countries.[22]

---

[21] See Taser International, press releases: Korean Airlines Selects Advanced Taser for Use on All Aircraft, March 27, 2002; United Airlines and Mesa Airlines Apply to Transportation Security Administration to Use Advanced Taser M26 for In-Flight Aircraft Security, January 21, 2003; Taser International, Inc. Commends Greek Police Special Forces on Use of Advanced Taser M26 to Arrest Turkish Airlines Flight 160 Hijacker, April 1, 2003, at http://phx.corporate-ir.net/phoenix.zhtml?c=129937&p=irol-news Article+ID=422451+highlight.

[22] James Campbell, Taser Guns May Be an Alternative, but Not a Panacea, *Houston Chronicle*, July 12, 2004, p. B9; Alex Berenson, As Police Use of Tasers Soars, Questions over Safety Emerge, *New York Times*, July 18, 2004, p. A1 (noting fifty deaths following taser shocking); Eric M. Koscove, The Taser Weapon: A New Emergency Medicine Problem, 14 *Annals of Emergency Medicine* No. 12, December 1985, p. 1205; Amnesty International, United States of America: Excessive and Lethal Force? Amnesty International's Concerns about Deaths and Ill-Treatment Involving Police Use of Tasers, November 30, 2004.

Pepper Spray. The search for a more-effective-yet-safer chemical means of crowd control has inspired generations of alchemists and inventors; the newly emerging leading technology employs oleoresin capsicum (OC), derived from natural cayenne pepper plants, or PAVA, an even more powerful synthetic equivalent. Available in spray cans that project to a distance of twelve feet or more, OC already has earned such a reputation for effectiveness that it has very largely displaced earlier CS and CN chemical sprays for use by police agencies in the United States. Likewise, U.S. military peacekeepers and MPs carried pepper spray on missions in Rwanda, Haiti, and Somalia.

Vendors and advocates contend that pepper spray acts much more quickly (a two-second burst can inflame the mucous membranes of the eyes, nose, throat, and lungs, causing pain, temporary blindness and shortness of breath for fifteen to sixty minutes), and that it will safely incapacitate even individuals under the influence of alcohol or drugs that would put them beyond the reach of other chemicals. Proponents claim a success rate of up to 90 percent for OC – saying the spray accomplishes its disabling objective that often in field applications – and identify reductions in injuries to both officers and suspects, and decreases in complaints about police use of excessive force, in jurisdictions where pepper spray has been adopted.

Again, critics contest the effectiveness of the substance (asserting that a substantial percentage of people are not restrained by it, and that close proximity is required to apply the spray accurately), its safety (noting dozens of in-custody deaths associated with OC use), and its propensity for inappropriate use (e.g., against individuals who are not resisting or are already under restraint). The ACLU has challenged OC patterns of use, asserting that police have come to rely upon the spray for mere convenience, rather than necessity, and that statistics suggest it may be used disproportionately against African Americans.[23]

Acoustic Rays. The concept of sound as a tool of battle goes back to Joshua's trumpets in the Biblical battle of Jericho, and in the modern era, a variety of concepts for acoustic rays were among the most evocative early NLW candidate technologies.

One such apparatus would emit inaudible, invisible sound waves to a distance of perhaps one hundred yards from a parabolic dish mounted on top of a jeep or Humvee that also carried the power source. The infrasound pulse would penetrate the target's body, disrupting internal organs (stomach, lungs, etc.) with unfamiliar harmonics, inducing uncontrollable nausea. The victim would have no choice but to retreat – or to fall down with paralyzing sickness, which would ebb once the originating wave source was removed. The acoustic waves would propagate efficiently even through dust, fog, or smoke, and even penetrate buildings. Early tests validated the principle (targets were rendered unfit for combat or any other concerted action), but developers to date have been unable to craft a suitably directional device – the acoustic beam fans out broadly from the emitting source, affecting anyone nearby, both friendly as well as opposing forces. Still, some imagine that such a system could be realized, perhaps to protect buildings from outsiders, or to safeguard ships in port against underwater scuba divers.

---

[23] Boyd, supra note 20 (calling OC "the less-than-lethal weapon of choice for US police"); Pepper Spray, Inc., www.peppersprayinc.com; Association of Defensive Spray Manufacturers, http://pepperspray.org; Jami Onnen, Oleoresin Capsicum, report for International Association of Chiefs of Police, June 1993; American Civil Liberties Union of Southern California, Pepper Spray: A Magic Bullet under Scrutiny, fall 1993; Associated Press, Black Leaders Urge Pepper Spray Ban, *Charlotte Observer*, November 4, 1997, p. 4C (between 1990 and 1997, eighty-four people died in police custody after being sprayed with chemicals; some allege a racial pattern in whom police spray with OC); National Institute of Justice, Office of Justice Programs, The Effectiveness and Safety of Pepper Spray, Research for Practice, April 2003.

Other possible applications of long-range sound waves (audible or inaudible) could be directly to inflict intolerable pain upon hostile persons, compelling them to retreat – but doing so would jeopardize hearing, possibly resulting in permanent damage. Discriminate targeting is also a difficult challenge, and even strong sound waves would be subject to relatively easy countermeasures, if ear protection devices were available to the targets. Britain and Israel already have deployed such high-decibel "acoustic cannon" systems, denominated "Curdler" and "Screamer," respectively, to disperse civilian crowds of protesters with a range of four hundred meters. Another concept would seek "acoustic bullets" – high-powered low-frequency blasts – to create an impact wave that would bowl over the targeted persons; again, a persistent hurdle has been the difficulty of achieving a system capable of propagating a coherent, accurate concussive force to suitable ranges.[24]

Directed Energy Heat Ray. Greater success has been earned by a facially similar device that employs millimeter energy waves instead of acoustic waves. Here a mobile prototype (denominated "Active Denial System" [ADS] or "Vehicle-Mounted Active Denial System" [VMADS]) has been thoroughly tested by the U.S. Air Force Research Laboratory in the New Mexico desert over a period of more than a decade at a cost of $50 million and is approaching the stage of operational deployment.

The invisible millimeter wave – effective at the speed of light to a remarkable range of a kilometer or more – stimulates the nerve endings in human skin, but penetrates only one-sixty-fourth of an

---

[24] Jürgen Altmann, Acoustic Weapons: Myths and Reality, in Dando, supra note 16, ch. 6 (arguing that reports about the power of acoustic weapons are overstated); Jürgen Altmann, Non-Lethal Weapons Technologies: The Case for Independent Scientific Analysis, in Nick Lewer (ed.), *The Future of Non-Lethal Weapons: Technologies, Operations, Ethics, and Law* (2002), pp. 112, 117–19.

inch. It almost immediately produces a powerful sensation of heat – as if the person were touching a hot light bulb – but does not, in fact, burn the skin or inflict any injury. The targeted person cannot resist the pain – one must involuntarily recoil or avoid the searing stimulus – but the punishment ceases as soon as the person withdraws or the device is aimed elsewhere. It is effective even through heavy clothing; the utility of other avoidance tactics (hiding behind a mirror or layers of wet towels, for example) is still being explored.

Proponents foresee using the millimeter wave to "clear a space" – to compel a crowd to abandon a contested area – or at least to differentiate between civilians or others who might just be "hangers-on" in a mob versus those more determined and prepared individuals who might constitute a real threat. Rigorous human effects testing has confirmed the safety and effectiveness of the system across a wide range of situations.

Four to six of the ADS devices are being mounted onto armored vehicles denominated "Sheriffs," and if all components can be integrated smoothly, they will be rushed into service in Iraq as early as 2006, to help scatter crowds and root out insurgent fighters. A future airborne iteration of ADS might be mounted on an AC-130 gunship for close air support and force protection missions.[25]

Chemical Calmatives or Malodorants. Additional chemical anti-personnel systems are also under consideration. The "holy grail" for researchers here would be a chemical that produced an immediate incapacitating effect but inflicted no lasting harm and was safe and

---

[25] U.S. Air Force, Fact Sheet: Active Denial System: Advanced Concept Technology Demonstration, February 2003 (noting that $9 million has been invested in human effects testing of the ADS over the past eleven years); CFR 3, supra note 8, at 25; Mihm, supra note 10, at 38.

effective for the full range of human populations – but that goal is likely to continue to prove as elusive as the real holy grail itself. The unavoidable problem is the range of human physiology: a dose that would be just barely sufficient to generate the intended effect on one person would be simultaneously too much for someone else (causing death or lasting injury) and too little for a third person (not sufficing to ensure disability). Even in a closely controlled and monitored setting such as a hospital operating room, the proper amount of anesthetic can vary in dramatic and unpredictable ways; when police or military authorities confront a crowd that includes young, healthy kidnappers and infirm civilians, the proper amount of chemicals to apply becomes hopelessly inexact.

Nonetheless, a pharmacopeia of candidate chemicals is under exploration, including some that "becalm" a targeted person (rendering him or her listless, disoriented, or unconscious) and "malodorants" (substances that simply smell so bad that people – other than those with preequipped with a specialized breathing apparatus – feel compelled to escape). In a similar vein, chemical dyes or markers might be applied remotely to indelibly designate particular persons in a crowd, singling them out for later identification and arrest.

Again, the utility of these concoctions is hotly debated; some opponents doubt that a truly safe and effective disabling chemical can ever be created. Moreover, the ready availability of effective self-protective devices (e.g., gas masks) decreases the potential value of chemicals in many situations. And as noted in Chapter 3, severe legal constraints impede the military application of chemical weapons.[26]

---

[26] See, e.g., Alexander Future War, supra note 20, at 76–80; Committee for an Assessment of Non-Lethal Weapons Science and Technology, Naval Studies Board, Division on Engineering and Physical Sciences, National Research Council, National Academies, An Assessment of Non-Lethal Weapons Science and Technology, National Academies Press (2003) (hereinafter National Research Council) pp. 27–8 (concluding that "Calmatives

Projectile Netting. NLW capabilities tackle antivehicle missions, as well as antipersonnel missions, and one of the most vexing cross-cutting demands is the challenge of stopping a fleeing or oncoming person, car, truck, boat, or airplane without inflicting permanent harm. A family of nascent capabilities seeks to employ netting of different composition and strength for these tasks. For example, a small antipersonnel version could be fired from a shotgun-like arm, flying out to ensnare a person in inescapable but nondamaging rope bindings. Instead of relying upon pain or injury to subdue a target, sheer physical entanglement cuts off his or her mobility.

A larger, stronger version could tackle the job of stopping a car or truck – possibly driven by a terrorist carrying explosives, but also possibly transporting a family of innocent civilians who did not recognize or understand signs and orders to stop. One model, denominated Portable Vehicle-Arresting Barrier, could be embedded in a roadway near a contested military checkpoint and is portable enough to be transported by police to a highway ahead of a fleeing vehicle. It relies upon polyethylene ropes and netting to entangle a vehicle's tires and undercarriage, and is capable of stopping a seventy-five hundred pound truck traveling at forty-five miles per hour, within a distance of two hundred feet.

Trailing that device in the development sequence is the Running Gear Entanglement System, a waterborne mechanism that the Coast Guard, for example, might use to interdict speedy cigarette boats suspected of drug trafficking. If the suspect is fast enough to outrun law enforcement cutters, and the officials are constrained not to employ deadly gunfire in ambiguous circumstances, a neat alternative might be to launch a netting that could capture the

---

represent a class of chemical substances that offer strong potential as effective NLWs"); Charles "Sid" Heal, The Quest for the "Magic Bullet," in Malcolm Dando, supra note 16, ch. 4.

target's propellers, forcing the craft to stop for boarding and inspection.

Antimateriel Biological and Chemical Agents. Modern biotechnology and chemistry suggest a variety of other capabilities that might be adapted to police or military NLW missions. Genetically engineered microbes can be imagined – whether they can actually be created on a practical scale is still an open question – to degrade the petroleum in an enemy's repositories, corrode rubber tires and gaskets on enemy vehicles, abrade moving parts, or perform other similar mischief. A particularly tantalizing image is metal "embrittlement" agents or other supercaustic chemicals, which hypothetically could be spread surreptitiously by aerosol or liquid onto enemy tanks or other equipment, rendering them (unbeknownst to the enemy) much more fragile and vulnerable in combat.[27]

Again, critics question the feasibility of these devices (could microbiological processes work quickly enough to have a measurable effect on combat), their controllability (might they proliferate beyond the intended target area, befouling our own materiel), and their military value (if our agents could get close enough to enemy forces to deploy these devices, why not simply use ordinary explosives).

---

[27] Note that antimateriel applications of this sort would not be "temporary" or "reversible" in the sense demanded of antipersonnel NLWs (although in some scenarios, perhaps the affected vehicle could be repaired, and parts replaced, more quickly than if it had been struck by a conventional explosive bomb). The notion of "non-lethal" nonetheless applies to these devices that cause catastrophic, permanent damage to targeted equipment, buildings, and other substances, because they operate via unconventional, novel routes, rather than explosions or gross physical deformities, and programs in pursuit of these concepts are sponsored by the JNLWD. DoD Directive 3000.3, supra note 1, at 3.1; Joint Non-Lethal Weapons Directorate, U.S. Marine Corps, Joint Concept for Non-Lethal Weapons, January 5, 1998, p. 8.

Miscellaneous Non-Lethal Weapons Concepts. This abbreviated roster of extant and nascent NLW capabilities merely scratches the surface – enthusiasts have compiled inventories of two dozen or more NLW notions in varying stages of development.[28] Some seem hopelessly ambitious, others may be of questionable military or police value – but work is progressing apace. In one program, researchers are exploring high-power microwave or electromagnetic pulse (EMP) devices that might be able to turn off or burn out the electrical system of an approaching car or truck at a standoff distance, so that even if the driver refused directions to stop at a checkpoint, the vehicle could be halted before it got too close. The microwaves have no injurious effect on people, but so far, the concept works only against modern computer-assisted cars, not against the older, simpler iterations of vehicles that would be more readily employed against American forces by terrorists in developing countries. Another mysterious technology would employ a "vortex ring generator" to create invisible rotating energy circles (akin to smoke rings, but with a tremendous punch) that could be propagated through the air at fifty to seventy meters per second to collide with targeted individuals.

Some of the new technologies may provide a modern twist to old problems. For example, a "ring airfoil grenade" might provide a new form of non-lethal bullet. It would be an aerodynamic, soft rubberlike ring designed to spin in flight after being shot from

---

[28] For sketches of the array of candidate NLW concepts, see Nick Lewer and Neil Davison, Non-Lethal Technologies – An Overview, *Disarmament Forum*, No. 1, 2005, p. 36; Dando, supra note 16, Brian Rappert, *Non-Lethal Weapons as Legitimizing Forces? Technology, Politics and the Management of Conflict*, 2003; Nick Lewer (ed.), *The Future of Non-Lethal Weapons: Technologies, Operations, Ethics, and Law*, 2002; Committee for an Assessment of Non-Lethal Weapons Science and Technology, Naval Studies Board, Division on Engineering and Physical Sciences, National Research Council, National Academies, *An Assessment of Non-Lethal Weapons Science and Technology*, 2003.

a ordinary-looking firearm, making it accurate to forty to sixty meters, with a stunning – but not lethal – impact. Another modest advance would be newer generations of "flash-bangs" – multisensory grenade-like devices that an assault team could use to temporarily stun barricaded targets through dazzling lights, loud noises, and foul smells, enabling the authorities to seize control of the situation in the moments of chaos. Other forms of momentarily blinding laser "dazzlers" might also be improved, to provide a short-term advantage for a police or military assault squad. Yet another program suggests creating a vast quantity of opaque (but breathable) aqueous foam – like an instant wall of dense soap bubbles – to disorient and subdivide a crowd.

The candidate NLW technologies could be combined in all sorts of ingenious ways. A plastic bullet can be contrived to carry a packet of OC, to explode into a disabling spray upon impact; projectile netting might be outfitted to carry an electrical charge, to further encumber the victim. As Malcolm Wiener has noted, these combined effects can complicate at opponent's task: even if a target of police or military forces came to the fray equipped to negate one form of NLW, it is difficult to imagine a terrorist or street mob armed simultaneously with gas masks, earplugs, body armor, shield mirrors, sand to throw on slippery foam, and medications to combat nausea.[29] On the other hand, some combined NLW effects can prove treacherous: the electrical charge from a taser can ignite the solvent used to propel pepper spray or CS gas, resulting in setting the target afire.

D. NON-LETHAL MISSIONS

Where did all this sudden interest in NLWs come from? What has inspired so many recent investigations into novel non-lethal

[29] Malcolm Wiener, private communication, September 20, 2004.

concepts? This section describes a few of the "classic" scenarios in which military and police officials imagine that new capabilities might prove useful – and superior to existing arms that too often leave them inadequate flexibility and deftness.

Military Scenarios. The first element animating the newfound military curiosity about NLWs comes from "military operations other than war" (MOOTW). American forces these days are increasingly deployed abroad to perform functions that differ in significant respects from the traditional notion of large-scale, force-on-force combat. Peacekeeping operations, for example, may emphasize the task of separating two wary combatants, providing a disengagement barrier between them, to deter further fighting. An armed U.S. military force sometimes may provide the best such bulwark, but any exercise of traditional lethal force – even in self-defense – might trigger an outbreak of the very hostilities we are seeking to avoid.

Similarly, other military missions require a forceful presence, but with a discreet touch. If U.S. troops are performing a humanitarian mission – providing protection for a relief mission that is distributing meals and medical services to a war-ravaged locale, for example – it hardly makes sense to train deadly force upon the very people we are trying to aid, but what should the troops do if the populace, growing weary of their plight, riots at the sight of a food truck?

To take a slight variant, imagine U.S. troops dispatched into a volatile country to provide protection for a U.S. embassy or base, or to help evacuate American civilians who have fallen into harm's way in the midst of a coup d'état or a martial law situation. What should they do if their position is approached by a large and unruly crowd – perhaps a mob composed mostly of unarmed (but angry) civilians, sprinkled with a handful of more determined (and armed) provocateurs? In particular, what should the U.S. soldiers do if a shot is fired? Loosening indiscriminate lethal force upon the crowd is obviously unacceptable – but so is doing nothing, while allowing the perpetrators a safe haven to keep firing.[30]

The first concerted application of significant NLWs in modern military history came in just this sort of situation, where civilians and fighters were thoroughly mixed, and where U.S. forces could not adequately differentiate between threatening and nonthreatening groups aligned against them. In 1995 the 13th Marine Expeditionary Unit was assigned the daunting mission of covering the withdrawal of twenty-five hundred United Nations peacekeepers from chaotic Somalia, providing protection against native warlords and disorganized military and paramilitary units as the multinational force was extracted.

Lieutenant General Anthony C. Zinni boldly decided to include a variety of NLWs in the Marines' training and equipment for this operation United Shield, and his departure from standard operating procedures garnered a substantial amount of publicity. Among the unconventional tools deployed to Somalia were sticky foam (used to create temporary, immediate barriers), caltrops (sharp-edged pyramids that could puncture the tires of vehicles following too closely), flash-bang and stinger grenades, low-kinetic-energy bullets (firing beanbags or wooden plugs), laser dazzlers and target designators, and chemical riot control agents.

---

[30] A similarly urgent need is for the development of new NLW systems to help protect U.S. Navy vessels in foreign ports, to avoid another catastrophe such as the attack on the *USS Cole* in Yemen in October 2000. Advocates imagine a "layered" system embracing both non-lethal and lethal mechanisms, in which increasingly emphatic warnings and deterrence measures are engaged as unknown vessels (including, of course, even small and apparently innocent boats) approach the ship. National Research Council, supra note 26, at 16–17, 115–18.

The mission was a resounding success, due at least in part to the deterrent effect of the unfamiliar non-lethal arms, which allowed the Marines safely to protect themselves and the UN forces, even against hordes of people pressing around them with mixed motives. The UN forces successfully completed their withdrawal from Mogadishu, and Zinni, reflecting upon the precedent-setting use of NLW, concluded, "I think the whole nature of warfare is changing."[31]

A rather different motivation for NLWs also has emerged even in the context of full-scale traditional combat. Since World War II, the United States and its allies have fought limited wars, for limited purposes – even during the most intense combat, we contemplate what we will do once the shooting stops, and we hope to create the most advantageous postconflict environment. In particular, it often turns out that the United States will help reconstruct the erstwhile enemy, and we therefore share an interest in preserving intact as much as possible of the country's infrastructure. In short, we fight to win the war as quickly as possible, but we also keep one eye on winning the peace, and that latter process is often materially assisted by avoiding cataclysmic damage to critical roads, bridges, power plants, and the like.

NLWs can provide a rare mechanism for pursuing both sets of goals simultaneously – preventing the enemy from using a resource to our detriment during the war, but also preserving it so it can more quickly and easily be restored to full functioning to assist the civilian economy in postwar recovery. For example, it was largely for that reason, during the 1999 fighting in Yugoslavia, that the United States

---

[31] Quoted in Rick Atkinson, Lean, Not-So-Mean Marines Set for Somalia, *Washington Post*, February 25, 1995, p. A22. See also National Research Council, supra note 26, at 53; Eric Schmitt, Now, to the Shores of Somalia with Beanbag Guns and Goo, *New York Times*, February 15, 1995, p. A10.

refrained from attacking a crucial electrical switching installation in Belgrade with ordinary explosive ordnance. The facility was a legitimate military target – it provided power used by the armed forces – but its complete destruction also would have retarded restoration of normal services to civilians during and after that short conflict. The solution was a "soft kill" – dropping loads of carbon fiber strips onto the facility, in an attack that caused massive electrical short-circuits, putting the grid out of order (and thereby denying service to the military) but doing so in a fashion that was reversible relatively rapidly, facilitating the subsequent restoration of normal service for peaceful purposes.

NLWs, therefore, offer the possibility of multiple technologies available for a variety of modern military missions. They may find application in both tactical, short-range maneuvers (e.g., to facilitate the operations and self-protection of a small unit operating within a confined space) and in strategic, long-range operations (e.g., to help prepare the battlespace by compromising the integrity of enemy assets such as airstrips and railyards long before assaulting troops arrive on the scene).

Police Scenarios. Like the military, police[32] frequently are confounded by sensitive and complex use-of-force situations. They may need, for example, to control an unruly crowd of demonstrators and to prevent them from destroying property – but they obviously do not want to apply deadly force. They may need to pursue a fleeing felon – but high-speed car chases are notoriously dangerous in

---

[32] For purposes of this book, the category of "police" refers generally to the full spectrum of domestic law enforcement and corrections officials, including a variety of federal, state, and local authorities such as sheriffs, U.S. Marshals, Secret Service, Federal Bureau of Investigation, Bureau of Alcohol, Tobacco, Firearms and Explosives, Drug Enforcement Administration, and others who perform cognate missions. It also can include National Guard units and military personnel performing temporary missions of assistance to civil authorities.

urban areas. They may need to subdue a belligerent, armed person, especially someone intoxicated by alcohol or drugs, impeding compliance with verbal instructions – but ordinary measures of force can quickly become excessive. They frequently need to transport a dangerous person – dangerous to himself, to the officers, and even to their squad car – to a station or jail. Corrections institutions, too, are another plausible venue for law enforcement NLWs – prison disruptions and riots can be disastrous, and conventional weaponry alone may not provide a sufficiently discriminating response inside confined spaces.

In the worst scenarios, police may confront a hostage/barricade situation, in which an armed individual or group is positioned in the midst of, and shielded by, innocents. There, extreme measures of force may be required to apprehend and disarm the antagonists and free the victims – as well as to protect the police themselves – but too often bystanders may be jeopardized by a lethal crossfire.

With all that background, police forces across the country have a much greater wealth of experience in operating NLWs – at least the low-tech, inexpensive variants. Pepper spray, tasers, rubber bullets, and the like have become staples in the inventories of many jurisdictions, and, in general, local police seem quite pleased with the technological gap-fillers.

But the available NLW arsenal for law enforcement is far from adequate. As far back as Lyndon Johnson's administration, the U.S. government recognized the need for, and committed itself to develop and procure, safer and more effective mechanisms of crowd control:

Revolvers and nightsticks are clearly inadequate for the many different crises faced by the police. New weapons and chemicals – effective but causing no permanent injury – have been and are being developed. But too little is now known about their potential to preserve order while protecting lives.

Too little is known about their limitations. I am instructing the Director of the Office of Science and Technology, working with the Attorney General and law enforcement officials, to study these new weapons and chemicals and other new technologies in crime control. The results of this study will be made available to enforcement agencies throughout the country.[33]

Nonetheless, despite immense technological growth in so many other sectors of modern American life, domestic law enforcement officials often still feel that they are equipped little differently than their nineteenth-century predecessors such as Wyatt Earp – if somebody will not heed their verbal commands, the only real recourse is to a firearm.

In sum, NLWs carry the promise of important new capabilities for police and military units in the twenty-first century. It is difficult to predict at this point which of these novel systems will ultimately prove to be "revolutionary technologies" and which will be revealed as dead ends, but it is clear that something important is already occurring.

The most obvious and familiar manifestations of NLW innovation may be the least provocative: caltrops, flash-bangs, projectile netting, and the like are useful, but they can be improved only so much further, and they do not raise the most pressing questions of law, tactics, or ethics. Similarly, the JNLWD has basically concluded, and the Department of Justice seems to concur, that the wave of the future for NLWs does not feature further refinements on kinetic energy projectiles – we have, for the most part, gone about as far as

---

[33] Lyndon Johnson, The Challenge of Crime to Our Society, HR Doc. No. 250, 90th Cong; 2nd session, February 7, 1968, at 14. See also Report of the National Advisory Commission on Civil Disorders, 1968, at 330, 492. ("For the most part, the police faced with urban disorders last summer had to rely on two weapons – a wooden stick and a gun. Our police departments today require a range of physical force with which to restrain and control both more humanely and more effectively." "The federal government should undertake an immediate program to test and evaluate nonlethal weapons and related control equipment for use by police and control forces.")

we can with plastic, rubber, and wooden bullets – so future iterations of blunt trauma munitions will be noteworthy only if they can offer appreciably greater range, safety, or reliability. For very different reasons, the realm of chemical and biological NLWs proceeds under a cloud. As discussed in the next chapter, international obligations and domestic statutes put biological weapons (BWs) entirely off limits, and there is little reason to want to disturb those strictures to proceed with non-lethal biological or toxin weapons designed for antipersonnel applications. The notion of antimateriel BWs (bugs that would quickly and perhaps covertly degrade metal armor, petroleum products, or machine parts) still seems far-fetched. The Chemical Weapons Convention likewise takes most military applications of toxic chemicals off the table; despite the lingering notion that chemical combat (especially non-lethal chemical combat) might be useful and even humane in some circumstances, the global consensus strongly moves in the opposite direction. Riot control agents – possibly including a wide range of new calmative, malodorant, and other concoctions – remain available for domestic law enforcement purposes, as well as for a host of "military operations other than war." The prospect of leakage from permitted chemical NLW operations into treaty-forbidden practices is, however, a serious issue, so again, there is a cap on the future utility of non-lethal chemicals.

The realm of directed energy NLWs seems to be the most tantalizing prospect. The VMADS millimeter wave heat ray, the possibility of improved acoustic systems, and the invention of comparable mechanisms yet to come suggest the ability to affect people, buildings, and objects at standoff distances; that would truly provide a revolutionary new capability. The technology is not yet battle-tested – the new Sheriff system planned for deployment in Iraq soon may provide the first operational evaluation – but already there is reason to be hopeful that the new NLWs can make a useful contribution in the most difficult engagements.

No one should be too sanguine about the promise of NLWs – there have been plenty of instances in which a vaunted new military technology conspicuously failed to live up to its advance billing. And even advocates grumble that progress has been slower than anticipated in bringing advanced NLW concepts from the drawing board into the field.

What is clear, however, is the large and growing effort now being devoted to the enterprise. Government-sponsored research is progressing, loosely coordinated between the Department of Defense (which brings more money to the table) and the Department of Justice (which draws upon more extensive experience in operating NLWs through state and local police forces). Even more, private enterprise has begun to adopt the NLW mission with alacrity and enthusiasm, and human inventiveness guarantees that candidate non-lethal programs of all sorts, based on a wide variety of physical mechanisms, will be explored and tested, and perhaps deployed and utilized, in the coming years.

THREE

The Law of Non-Lethal Weapons

Both international and domestic law fail to make adequate provision for non-lethal weapons. The existing standards were crafted, of course, with other stimuli in mind, and contemporary treaties, statutes, and other legal tools, for the most part have not yet been adapted to the unprecedented stresses and opportunities of the modern capabilities. Still, there are some shreds of law that do regulate the emerging world of NLWs – for better or worse. This chapter explores three topics. First is the international context: treaties and customary rules that govern selected aspects of the weaponry wielded by American and other armed forces. Second (more briefly) is the domestic U.S. statutory law that forecloses one important potential avenue of NLW research and development, regarding biological weapons. Third is the domestic U.S. constitutional and other law regulating police use of weapons, including NLW capabilities, highlighting the evolving jurisprudence in the field of "excessive force."

A. INTERNATIONAL LAW ON NON-LETHAL WEAPONS

Only a few treaties deal directly with NLWs, and they do so in a distinctly incomplete fashion, but those few exemplars are worth exploring.

Chemical Weapons Convention. The first noteworthy international agreement relevant to our story is the 1993 Convention on the Prohibition of the Development, Production, Stockpiling and Use of Chemical Weapons and on Their Destruction (Chemical Weapons Convention or CWC).[1] The CWC is a comprehensive edict against a particularly obnoxious form of combat, and it has attracted 168 parties, reflecting the world's consensus that this hideous scourge is to be avoided absolutely.[2] At the same time, however, the scope of the treaty's prohibitions must not be too broad: because of the phenomenon of "dual capability" – many of the same chemical substances, processes, and equipment can be used both for weapons and for plastics, paints, fertilizers, and insecticides across the full spectrum of the global civilian economy – the treaty must be careful not to disrupt essential patterns of commercial activity.

The CWC therefore defines its applicable coverage with care. A "chemical weapon" includes "toxic chemicals and their precursors, except where intended for purposes not prohibited under this Convention, as long as the types and quantities are consistent with such purposes."[3] This leads to two other essential definitions. First, a "toxic chemical" is "Any chemical which through its chemical

---

[1] Convention on the Prohibition of the Development, Production, Stockpiling and Use of Chemical Weapons and on Their Destruction, opened for signature January 13, 1993, S. Treaty Doc. 103–21, 1974 U.N.T.S. 3, 32 I.L.M. 800, entered into force April 29, 1997 (hereinafter CWC). See also Protocol for the Prohibition of the Use in War of Asphyxiating, Poisonous or Other Gases, and of Bacteriological Methods of Warfare, signed June 17, 1925, 26 U.S.T. 571, 94 L.N.T.S. 65 (Geneva Protocol) (earlier instrument outlawing the use of chemical weapons in particular circumstances, but not forbidding their development and possession).

[2] See www.opcw.org/html/db/members_frameset.html, last visited June 6, 2005. The United States, as well as all the other permanent members of the UN Security Council, are members.

[3] CWC, supra note 1, art. II.1 (a). A chemical weapon consists of two components: the lethal or non-lethal agent (e.g., sarin nerve gas or OC pepper spray) and the munition or device (e.g., a bomb, mine, or spray tank) that is used to contain the agent, transport it to the target, and disperse it. For present purposes, we are concerned only with the agent, although the CWC tightly regulates the delivery systems too. Ibid. at art. II.1 (b) and (c).

action on life processes can cause death, *temporary incapacitation or permanent harm to humans or animals.*"[4] The most important such toxic chemicals are identified on a series of three "schedules" annexed to the treaty and are the subject of a detailed verification regime to ensure compliance, incorporating elaborate reporting and inspection requirements.[5]

Second, the term "purposes not prohibited under this convention" includes an array of industrial, agricultural, medical, and other peaceful purposes, as well as "Law enforcement including domestic riot control purposes."[6] This last exemption then requires the introduction of an additional set of crucial terms and constraints. Under the CWC, "Each State Party undertakes not to use riot control agents as a method of warfare."[7] Riot control agent is then defined as "Any chemical not listed in a Schedule, which can produce rapidly in humans sensory irritation or disabling physical effects which disappear within a short time following termination of exposure."[8]

---

[4] CWC, supra note 1, art. II.2 (emphasis added).
[5] CWC, supra note 1, art. II.2; Annex on Chemicals; and Annex on Implementation and Verification.
[6] CWC, supra note 1, art. II.9. The CWC does not bar the use of small quantities of chemical weapons agents for "protective purposes" such as in experiments designed for the development of improved anti-CW self-defense equipment such as "gas masks." Ibid. art. II.9 (b). However, chemicals listed on schedule 1 of the treaty (the most dangerous substances – those toxic chemicals, and their precursors, that have previously been developed or produced as chemical weapons) may be used only for a narrower range of peaceful purposes, not including law enforcement or riot control purposes. CWC, Verification Annex, Part VI.2; David Fidler, Law Enforcement under the Chemical Weapons Convention: Interpretation of Article II.9(d) of the Chemical Weapons Convention in Regard to the Use of Toxic Chemicals for Law Enforcement Purposes, memorandum to FAS Working Group, April 24, 2003 (hereinafter Fidler FAS).
   Likewise, the treaty recognizes the fact that many ordinary weapons rely upon substances – such as gunpowder or rocket fuel – that might fit the criteria of "toxic chemicals" in being harmful to humans, but those chemicals are not being used in combat in a fashion that exploits their toxic nature. The treaty therefore exempts "Military purposes not connected with the use of chemical weapons and not dependent on the use of the toxic properties of chemicals as a method of warfare." CWC at art. 9 (c).
[7] CWC, supra note 1, art. I.5.
[8] CWC, supra note 1, art. II.7.

The CWC further requires each party to declare the chemical name, structural formula, and registry number (although not the quantity produced, the location, or the purpose) of each chemical it holds for riot control purposes, and to update this information within thirty days of any change.[9]

The interplay of these terms and their net effect on non-lethal chemicals have been muddled and controversial – the suitability of riot control agents on the battlefield has been a legal, tactical, and political quagmire for decades predating and under the CWC. The United States has traditionally argued that riot control agents do not fit the criteria of "toxic chemicals" and are therefore not "chemical weapons" under the treaty. Accordingly, they may be produced, stockpiled, and deployed without limits, subject only to the restriction that they may not be used "as a method of warfare." Virtually all other parties and observers argue conversely, that riot control agents *are* toxic chemicals under the CWC, *are* chemical weapons, and thus may be held only in quantities and types appropriate for the articulated "peaceful purposes," as well as not being valid "as a method of warfare."[10]

Only small operational consequences may now remain in this legal brouhaha – the United States has emplaced severe internal restraints against even approaching any uses of riot control agents in the most contentious hypothetical cases. But what would be a use of chemicals, including non-lethal chemicals, as a prohibited "method of warfare"? Surely any employment against fighting forces would

---

[9] CWC, supra note 1, art. III.1 (e).
[10] Ernest Harper, A Call for a Definition of Method of Warfare in Relation to the Chemical Weapons Convention, 48 *Naval Law Review*, pp. 132, 134–43 (2001); David P. Fidler, The International Legal Implications of "Non-Lethal" Weapons, 21 *Michigan Journal of International Law*, fall 1999, pp. 51, 72–3; J. P. Winthrop, Preliminary Legal Review of Proposed Chemical-Based Nonlethal Weapons, Department of the Navy, Office of the Judge Advocate General, International & Operational Law Division, National Security Law Branch, November 30, 1997, pp. 16–19.

now be covered – such as the American applications of riot control agents during the Vietnam War to drive enemy soldiers out of underground bunkers or tunnels. A closer case might be "search and rescue" missions – if a pilot is downed behind enemy lines, would it be legal to use riot control agents to prevent local civilians from approaching his position, until a helicopter can extract him? Or what if an enemy is illegally using civilians as "human shields" – would it be an acceptable reprisal to employ a non-lethal gas that would incapacitate and disperse the entire crowd, permitting a more discrete application of deadly force against the perpetrators? Most plausibly on the "legal" side of the fence would be use of riot control agents in rear areas, away from the fighting, such as to control rioting civilians in occupied territory or interned enemy prisoners of war. Antimateriel chemical weapons – lethal or non-lethal – it is worth noting, are outside the scope of the CWC altogether.

David Fidler has argued for a narrow interpretation of the phrase "law enforcement including domestic riot control purposes" within the CWC's strictures allowing chemicals for "peaceful purposes." He asserts that the treaty permits a party to employ non-lethal chemicals to ensure compliance with its domestic legal strictures within its own territory and in areas subject to its jurisdiction, but does not authorize chemicals for extraterritorial enforcement of its domestic law or of international law. Furthermore, NLW chemicals could legitimately be applied by military forces in areas they occupy, or by authorized peacekeepers, for the law enforcement purpose of preserving public order and safety, but only against noncombatants.[11]

In contrast, Hays Parks has argued that the CWC's outlawing of riot control agents as a "method" of warfare is appreciably less

---

[11] Fidler FAS, supra note 6.

constricting than if the treaty had banned chemicals as a "means" of warfare. Under this analysis, the "methods" of warfare are broad policies, aimed at the strategic, operational level of war, while the "means" of warfare operate at the tactical level. The contemplated application of NLW chemicals on the battlefield would all be in discrete, specific, localized situations – as "means" of accomplishing a particular mission, not as broad-gauged "methods" of defeating an enemy state. Accordingly, the CWC should be interpreted to tolerate these particularized applications of NLW riot control agents.[12]

Current United States policy stands approximately midway between these two perspectives, as reflected in Executive Order 11850, promulgated by President Gerald Ford in 1975. There he asserted the right to use riot control agents in defensive military modes to save lives, such as in four specified situations: to control rioting prisoners of war, to counter enemy attacks that use civilians as shields, to rescue downed pilots, and to protect rear areas away from the fighting against riots and terrorists.[13] That position, despite its facial inconsistency with the CWC, has been frozen into U.S. law by the Senate's insistence upon retaining it during the treaty ratification process. But it is also clear that any application of even non-lethal chemicals in any near-battlefield circumstances would be politically, legally, and tactically risky; any such action would have to be authorized only by the uppermost echelons of the national command authority, and is unlikely to be tolerated.

The "bottom line" for assessing the impact of the CWC on possible use of non-lethal chemicals remains, therefore, shrouded in some

---

[12] Harper, supra note 10, at 154–5.
[13] Gerald R. Ford, Renunciation of Certain Uses in War of Chemical Herbicides and Riot Control Agents, Executive Order 11850, April 8, 1975, 3 CFR 980, 50 USC 1511, 40 *Fed Reg* 16187 (1975), 11 *Weekly Compilation of Presidential Documents* No. 15, p. 350.

uncertainty. Clearly, no chemicals, including non-lethal riot control agents, can be utilized "as a method of warfare." Equally clearly, any effort to test the limits of that prohibition – such as by considering possible applications of NLW riot control agents in near-combat situations – would be controversial and fraught with political and strategic peril. Most of the world would not accept as legitimate any meaningful introduction of NLW chemicals into a theater of war – and the eventual retaliation might overwhelm whatever temporary tactical advantage was obtained by the first user. The treaty does not similarly constrain law enforcement applications of non-lethal chemicals, but neither does it offer much assistance in attempting to segregate the military from the police applications in close cases.

Biological Weapons Convention. A similar, but less textually based, story emerges from analysis of the CWC's predecessor, the 1972 Convention on the Prohibition of the Development, Production and Stockpiling of Bacteriological (Biological) and Toxin Weapons and on Their Destruction (Biological Weapons Convention or BWC).[14] The BWC predated the CWC by two decades; reflecting its era, the earlier instrument is vastly shorter, lacking the richly detailed

---

[14] Convention on the Prohibition of the Development, Production and Stockpiling of Bacteriological (Biological) and Toxin Weapons and on Their Destruction, opened for signature April 10, 1972, 26 U.S.T. 583, 1015 U.N.T.S. 163 (hereinafter BWC). The treaty has been joined by 153 countries, including the United States and most of the other key players. See www.opbw.org, visited June 6, 2005.

The difference between a "chemical" weapon and a "biological" weapon is elusive. In general, a biological weapon (such as anthrax or smallpox) relies upon living creatures (usually microscopic) or infectious materials derived from them (or on artificially created analogues), which reproduce and cause a "disease" in the targeted person, plant, or animal. A chemical weapon (such as sarin or mustard gas), in partial contrast, uses a substance with direct toxic effects, generally not causing a communicable illness. A "toxin" weapon (such as rattlesnake venom or botulin) is a sort of middle ground – it employs poisonous substances extracted from living things or created in a laboratory. The CWC and BWC therefore overlap to some extent; the legal pigeonholes do not precisely correspond to the vagaries of nature.

definitions, schedules of covered substances, elaborate verification protocols, and consideration of diverse scenarios for possible legitimate uses of biological agents.

The BWC states simply "Each State Party to this Convention undertakes never in any circumstances to develop, produce, stockpile or otherwise acquire or retain . . . Microbial or other biological agents, or toxins whatever their origin or method of production, of types and in quantities that have no justification for prophylactic, protective or other peaceful purposes."[15] The treaty therefore applies equally to lethal and to non-lethal biological agents; it makes no special provision for conceivable biological "riot control agents" or other less-noxious breeds of bugs. The outstanding question – unadorned in the treaty's text – is whether the permission for "prophylactic, protective or other peaceful purposes" could be stretched to embrace microbes used for nonwar, but war-related or law enforcement, applications.

There is little real learning on this topic, and to date, little discussion of it; likewise, few people have systematically considered the possibility of genetically engineered microbes deliberately dispersed in an antimateriel role. The treaty mostly contemplates bugs and toxins that counteract living things, by causing a disease or interfering with life processes – how should it deal with supercaustics or super-biodegraders?

Convention on Certain Conventional Weapons. A third treaty reveals a different aspect of the emerging NLW story: how the world community sometimes deals with selected weaponry that it considers particularly loathsome, regardless of its non-lethal character. The 1980 Convention on Prohibitions or Restrictions on the Use

[15] BWC, supra note 14, art. I.

of Certain Conventional Weapons Which May Be Deemed to Be Excessively Injurious or to Have Indiscriminate Effects (Convention on Certain Conventional Weapons or CCW) governs, through a series of protocols that each party may opt to join separately, a Pandora's box of nasty or inhumane weapons such as landmines, booby traps, and incendiary devices.[16] Protocol IV to the treaty, concluded in 1995, confronts blinding laser weapons.

It is a response to the impending proliferation of laser devices of various sorts on the battlefield, where they can perform a number of functions, including range finding and target designating – and potentially blinding enemy soldiers. Under the protocol, "It is prohibited to employ laser weapons specifically designed, as their sole combat function or as one of their combat functions, to cause permanent blindness to unenhanced vision, that is to the naked eye or to the eye with corrective eyesight devices."[17] The Protocol deals only with systems that create irreversible, uncorrectable blindness, and that do so deliberately, specifying that "Blinding as an incidental or collateral effect of the legitimate military employment of laser systems, including laser systems used against optical equipment, is not covered by the prohibition of this Protocol."[18] Related laser systems, such as temporary "dazzlers," intended to disorient and cause transient loss of vision, are therefore outside the scope of the CCW.

---

[16] Convention on Prohibitions or Restrictions on the Use of Certain Conventional Weapons Which May Be Deemed to Be Excessively Injurious or to Have Indiscriminate Effects, Geneva, October 10, 1980, 1342 U.N.T.S. 137, 19 I.L.M. 1524 (1980) (hereinafter CCW). The treaty, to which ninety-four states are party, is an umbrella that now covers five distinct protocols, each of which may be joined individually: (1) prohibiting weapons that employ fragments undetectable in the human body via X-rays, (2) regulating the use of landmines, booby traps, and associated devices, (3) limiting weapons that are designed primarily to set fires or to cause burn injuries, (4) banning blinding laser weapons, and (5) addressing unexploded ordnance, the explosive remnants of war. See www.ccwtreaty.com, visited June 6, 2005.

[17] CCW, supra note 16, Protocol IV, art. 1.

[18] CCW, supra note 16, Protocol IV, art. 3.

Protocol IV thus reflects a growing shared global consensus – a sentiment appreciated in internal U.S. government policy, too[19] – that some forms of non-lethal combat are no longer acceptable. Even where the weapon is exquisitely "precise," in the sense of being targeted on a particular individual, and even when it results in "merely" a horrific injury, rather than in death, this particular non-lethal weapon is widely reviled, and now legally barred.

Law of Armed Conflict. In addition to these individual arms control treaties, the corpus of the law of armed conflict – both customary international law[20] and broadly applicable treaties – imposes other noteworthy limitations. These more general standards apply to all weapons, lethal and non-lethal alike, even those (such as the acoustic, electric, netting, and blunt trauma projectiles noted above) that have not yet been subjected to any dedicated treaty regime such as the CWC, BWC, or CCW.

The most important relevant criterion here is the imperative of avoiding "superfluous injury" and "unnecessary suffering."[21] Obviously, in any war, the parties deliberately inflict upon each other a great deal of pain – that is ordinarily inherent in the effort to bend the adversary to your will. But this agony is not without limit; the

---

[19] William J. Perry, Memorandum: DoD Policy on Blinding Lasers, January 17, 1997 (U.S. policy bars lasers "specifically designed to cause permanent blindness" but considers other types of laser systems (for detection, targeting, communications, etc.) "absolutely vital to our modern military."

[20] Customary international law "results from a general and consistent practice of states followed by them from a sense of legal obligation"; it binds countries independent of their participation in or avoidance of any particular treaty. American Law Institute, *Restatement of the Law: The Foreign Relations Law of the United States,* vol. 1, sec. 102 (2) (1986).

[21] Protocol Additional to the Geneva Conventions of August 12, 1949, and Relating to the Protection of Victims of International Armed Conflicts, June 8, 1977, 1125 U.N.T.S. 3 (hereinafter Protocol) (United States is not a party), article 35.2 ("It is prohibited to employ weapons, projectiles and materiel and methods of warfare of a nature to cause superfluous injury or unnecessary suffering"); Robin M. Coupland, Abhorrent Weapons and "Superfluous Injury or Unnecessary Suffering": From Field Surgery to Law, 315 *British Medical Journal* 1450, November 29, 1997.

legitimate objective is only to cause the enemy forces to submit – anything not designed and executed with that objective may be "unnecessary" and therefore "excessive" and illegal. Such a subjective standard, of course, is all but impossible to quantify and is often difficult to assess in any clear fashion at all – but the legal standard remains, and it is a touchstone against which any weapon, including each NLW, must be assessed.

A second crucial principle of international humanitarian law is that of discrimination or distinction: a valid weapon must be designed and employed in a fashion that enables it to be sufficiently precise, to attack only legitimate targets, differentiating, for example, between civilians and combatants, between a fighting force and those who are exempt from attack (e.g., medical personnel, individuals who are surrendering, or those already rendered *hors de combat* by injury or illness.) In some large measure, the inability to be sufficiently precise – the fact that they target wide areas, or cannot be adequately focused on belligerents – underpins the general antipathy to chemical or biological weapons (which may drift uncontrollably from a battlefield into a city), to antipersonnel landmines (which may remain active for years, exploding when triggered by a farmer tilling a field, long after the soldiers have marched away), and to nuclear weapons (which generate such massive destruction that distant noncombatants are inevitably implicated).

Corollary to these substantive standards is the procedural obligation for each country to assess carefully the legitimacy of each of its weapons. Under Protocol I Additional to the 1949 Geneva Conventions, a country is required, before deploying, and certainly before using, a new type of weapon to evaluate in good faith its conformity with the applicable rules of humanitarian law. It must ascertain, inter alia, that the device will not conflict with any applicable arms control treaty, that it will not cause unnecessary suffering, and that it can be deployed in an acceptably discriminatory fashion.[22] The United States, for example, routinely subjects new weapons proposals to legal scrutiny both at the stage at which research and development are being undertaken, and at the end of the evolutionary process, when production and deployment would be authorized. Non-lethal weapons from lasers to pepper spray to acoustic waves have survived this gauntlet.[23]

These critical precepts of the law of armed conflict are instructive for the evolving consideration of new non-lethal weapons, but they are not always as definitive as we might like in this context. In fact, many of the principles are problematic enough even within their traditional spheres, and they become even more strained when adapting to the unprecedented challenges of asymmetric warfare, modern superterrorism, and Military Operations in Urban Terrain (MOUT). For example, the fundamental requirements of distinction between civilians and combatants are muddied these days – if nonuniformed fighters mingle with a crowd, stir it into a frenzy, and push it forward toward a U.S. military base, at what point do the unarmed participants in the mob forfeit their protected status

[22] Protocol I, supra note 21, article 36 ("In the study, development, acquisition or adoption of a new weapon, means or method of warfare, a High Contracting Party is under an obligation to determine whether its employment would, in some or all circumstances, be prohibited by this Protocol or by any other rule of international law applicable to the High Contracting Party"); James C. Duncan, A Primer on the Employment of Non-Lethal Weapons, 45 *Naval Law Review* (1998), pp. 1, 26–9; Robin Coupland and Dominique Loye, Legal and Health Issues: International Humanitarian Law and the Lethality or Non-Lethality of Weapons, in Malcolm Dando (ed.), Non-Lethal Weapons: Technological and Operational Prospects, Jane's online special report (November 2000), sec. 7.6.

[23] Department of Defense Directive 5000.1, The Defense Acquisition System, May 12, 2003, sec. E1.1.15; Department of Defense Directive 3000.3, Policy for Non-Lethal Weapons, July 9, 1996, sec. 5.6.2. For examples of legal reviews of weapons, see Hugh R. Overholt and W. Hays Parks, Memorandum of Law: The Use of Lasers as Antipersonnel Weapons, September 29, 1988, reprinted in *Army Lawyer*, November 1988, p. 3; Joseph A. Rutigliano Jr., Memorandum for the Record: Legality of Oleoresin Capsicum (OC) under the Biological Weapons Convention and Its Implementing Legislation, JA02, October 22, 2002; J. P. Winthrop, Preliminary Legal Review of Proposed Acoustic Energy Non-Lethal Weapon Systems, Ser. 106/354, May 26, 1998.

by assuming a direct role in hostilities? Even more unsettling, if a
VMADS system is employed to clear civilians from an urban area –
surely a more benign alternative than destructive house-by-house
combat – how could those tactics square with the traditional prohibition against directly targeting civilians and their property?

B. U.S. LAW ON NON-LETHAL WEAPON DEVELOPMENT

In addition to these international law obligations, one domestic U.S.
statute relevant to non-lethal weapons must be highlighted. Under
the Biological Weapons Anti-Terrorism Act of 1989, as amended, the
United States is even more constrained regarding research and development of biological NLWs than are other members of the BWC
regime. This statute provides criminal penalties (fines, and up to
life imprisonment), injunctions, and forfeiture for developing, producing, stockpiling, transferring, acquiring, retaining, or possessing
any biological agent, toxin, or delivery system for use as a weapon,
except for "prophylactic, protective, or other peaceful purposes."[24]

The applicable terms are defined very broadly under the statute
("biological agent," for example, means "any microorganism" or
"infectious substance" or "any naturally occurring, bioengineered
or synthesized component").[25] It is clear, therefore, that non-lethal
as well as lethal substances are covered; that agents that attack
humans, animals, plants, or materiel are all equally barred; and that
there is no explicit exemption for anything like "law enforcement"
or "riot control agents" as under the CWC and its implementing
legislation. Whether any bio-related NLW programs could proceed
under the rubric of "prophylactic, protective or other peaceful
purposes" has not been tested. As a consequence, the Joint

[24] 18 U.S.C. 175–8.
[25] 18 U.S.C. 178.

Non-Lethal Weapons Directorate has stayed completely away from any form of biological NLWs.

C. U.S. LAW ON POLICE USE OF FORCE

In contrast to the first category above, in which the potential military applications of non-lethal weapons are constrained more by international agreements than by federal statutes, the potential police uses of NLWs are regulated largely by domestic law: the U.S. Constitution, federal and state legislation, and judicial cases. This book cannot survey the full array of state and federal legislative and judicial standards and interpretations reining in police violence, but a quick overview of the applicable rules may help elucidate the relevant principles that will guide law enforcement employment of non-lethal arms.[26]

The analysis begins with *Tennessee v. Garner*, the watershed 1985 case in which the Supreme Court decided that police may not use deadly force to prevent the flight of an apparently unarmed suspected felon, unless there is probable cause to believe that the suspect presents a significant threat of death or serious physical injury to the officer or others. The Fourth Amendment's prohibition on unreasonable seizures, the Court ruled, requires a balancing between the government's interest in effective law enforcement versus the individual's interest in liberty – and where a nondangerous individual is suspected of a serious, but relatively less hostile, offense, police could not constitutionally shoot him to prevent his escape.[27]

---

[26] See generally Michael Avery, David Rudovsky, and Karen M. Blum, *Police Misconduct: Law and Litigation* (3rd ed. 2003), sec. 2:18–2:22.

[27] Tennessee v. Garner, 471 U.S. 1, 9–11 (1985) (noting that "It is no doubt unfortunate when a suspect who is in sight escapes, but the fact that the police arrive a little late or are a little slower afoot does not always justify killing the suspect"). See also Vera Cruz v. Escondido, 139 F.3d 659 (9th Cir. 1997) (defining "deadly force").

This finding was extended four years later in *Graham v. Connor*, where the Court declared that *all* claims that law enforcement officers have employed excessive force (deadly or otherwise) in making an arrest, investigatory stop, or other seizure of a free citizen are to be evaluated under the Fourth Amendment's "reasonableness" standard. This delicate and difficult balancing requires careful attention to the amount, type, and duration of coercion applied, the importance of the police accomplishing their mission in this particular case, and the individual's loss of autonomy and bodily integrity.[28]

These cases helped inspire police forces across the country to explore alternatives to traditional lethal force with extra vigor – if ordinary firearms were now judged inappropriate for detaining many fleeing suspects, what additional tools might be available to assist in apprehending and subduing someone who was running or driving away?

In articulating these legal principles, the Court was careful to note that the determination of "reasonableness" in applying force posed a unique challenge for police and for judicial review: there was no formulaic "cookie-cutter" approach to these assessments, but each case had to be analyzed individually, under a "totality of the circumstances" approach. And the cops should be afforded a benefit of the doubt in close cases, especially where they were compelled to make split-second decisions under the pressure of incomplete information and potential hazard to themselves and others.[29]

---

[28] Graham v. Connor, 490 U.S. 386, 395–7 (1989) (explaining that the test is one of "objective reasonableness," in light of all the facts and circumstances known to the police at the time, rather than focusing on the motivations or the benign or hostile intentions of the officer).

[29] Garner, supra note 27, 471 U.S. at 8–9; Graham, supra note 28, 490 U.S. at 396–7 ("The calculus of reasonableness must embody allowance for the fact that police officers are often forced to make split-second judgments – in circumstances that are tense, uncertain, and rapidly evolving – about the amount of force that is necessary in a particular situation"); Bell v. Wolfish, 441 U.S. 520, 559 ("The test of reasonableness under the Fourth Amendment is not capable of precise definition or mechanical application").

Most notably, the caselaw has preserved a fine point of interpretation – and it is a point that is subtly different from the international legal standards noted above. That is, the police are constrained to use only "reasonable" levels of force – but not necessarily the "least intrusive" means. In a situation where it might be considered "reasonable" to choose any of a variety of possible approaches (and to employ accordingly varied levels and kinds of force), courts have not insisted that the officers start with the "lowest" level of compulsion (however that ladder of violence might be defined) and work their way up only when the less powerful tools prove unavailing. Of course, there may not be much leeway between the "lowest" level of force that would suffice to get the job done and a "reasonable" approach, but U.S. courts are now quite clear that the test is "reasonableness," not "minimal force."[30]

This somewhat murky Supreme Court guidance has failed, of course, to anticipate or resolve all subsequent controversies, and cases frequently test the application of various forms of lethal and non-lethal force. Regarding pepper spray, for example, there is no case law supporting the proposition that use of OC is per se excessive, but in selected circumstances, even this non-lethal form of police coercion may be deemed unreasonable. Where the targeted person is not resisting arrest or is sprayed repeatedly, or where police

---

[30] Forrester v. City of San Diego, 25 F.3d 804 (9th Cir. 1994). (Police used "pain compliance" techniques, via "nonchakus" [two wooden sticks, connected by a cord, wrapped around a demonstrator's wrist] to clear trespassing antiabortion protesters; when challenged by the assertion that it would have been more reasonable to drag or carry the protesters away, the 9th Circuit ruled, "Police officers, however, are not required to use the least intrusive degree of force possible. Rather, as stated above, the inquiry is whether the force that was used to effect a particular seizure was reasonable, viewing the facts from the perspective of a reasonable officer on the scene [citing *Graham*]. Whether officers hypothetically could have used less painful, less injurious, or more effective force in executing an arrest is simply not the issue.") Ibid. at 807–8.

fail to take appropriate measures to ameliorate the effects of the spray, courts find liability.[31] Likewise, police generally are allowed to employ taser electric guns, but in some circumstances, it may be unreasonable to do so.[32] Beanbag munitions (or other reduced impact blunt trauma projectiles) and police dogs are analyzed in a similar fashion: case-by-case determination will assess whether law enforcement relied unreasonably upon these tools.[33] Constraint mechanisms – handcuffs, hogties, etc. – also pose the same inquiry, and it will sometimes, but by no means always, be deemed reasonable to confine a particular individual in that ordinarily non-lethal fashion.[34]

---

[31] Vinyard v. Wilson, 311 F.3d 1340 (11th Cir. 2002) (unreasonable to use pepper spray against arrestee whose wrists were handcuffed behind her back and who had already been placed in a police car with protective screen between her and the officer); Park v. Shiflett, 250 F.3d 843 (4th Cir. 2001) (finding it excessive when police twice sprayed unresisting woman with pepper spray at very short range); LaLonde v. County of Riverside, 204 F.3d 947, 961 (9th Cir. 2000) ("the use of such weapons [e.g., pepper sprays, police dogs] may be reasonable as a general policy to bring an arrestee under control, but in a situation in which an arrestee surrenders and is rendered helpless, any reasonable officer would know that a continued use of the weapon or a refusal without cause to alleviate its harmful effects constitutes excessive force").

[32] Russo v. Cincinnati, 953 F.2d 1036 (6th Cir. 1992) (repeated use of taser was not excessive, even when the suspect lay at bottom of stairwell and posed no immediate threat to officers).

[33] On beaubag munitions, see Bell v. Irwin, 321 F.3d 637 (7th Cir. 2003) (record does not establish whether beanbag round should be classified as lethal, but where the alternative would have been use of ordinary firearms, the accused "should have thanked rather than sued the officers" who used the NLW munitions); Deorle v. Rutherford, 272 F.3d 1272 (9th Cir. 2001), cert. denied, 536 U.S. 958 (2002) (objectively unreasonable to shoot, even with beanbag round, unarmed, mentally disturbed man who posed no flight risk or threat to officers). On use of police dogs, see Jarrett v. Town of Yarmouth, 331 F.3d 140 (1 st Cir. 2003) (per curiam) (police dog trained in "bite and hold" technique does not constitute deadly or per se unreasonable force); Watkins v. City of Oakland, 145 F.3d 1087 (9th Cir. 1998) (dog is less dangerous than police baton, but where duration of dog's bite was excessive and police improperly encouraged continuation of attack, use of force was unreasonable).

[34] Avery, Rudovsky, and Blum, supra note 26, at sec. 2:19; Cruz v. City of Laramie, 239 F.3d 1183 (10th Cir. 2001) (use of "hog-tie" [binding ankles and wrists together behind the person's back] is not per se unreasonable, but is excessive where person's diminished capacity is apparent and makes use of constrictions more risky); Gutierrez v. City of San Antonio, 139 F.3d 441 (5th Cir. 1998) (hog-tying a substance-abusing person and placing him face down in the back seat of a police car was unreasonable).

Finally, courts are reluctant to second-guess police departments' procurement decisions regarding the type of equipment to field. Where a police force is armed only with customary lethal force, there is no constitutional violation, even in situations where NLWs would have enabled the use of better, more deft techniques. The administrative and budgetary choices not to purchase the equipment that would have created a particular – and, in hindsight, quite worthwhile – law enforcement capability do not rise to the level of unreasonable.[35]

Overall, then, the domestic U.S. law on police uses of force against nonincarcerated individuals relies upon an ineffable Fourth Amendment balancing test, demanding comparison of the competing values of personal liberty and governmental law enforcement. There can be no definitive formula for assessing the lawfulness of particular weaponry – lethal or non-lethal – as any tool could be wielded in an excessive fashion in a particular situation. But courts generally do provide a "margin of appreciation" for the predicament of law enforcement emergencies, and they do not require reliance upon the "least intrusive" NLW mechanism, so long as the actual force applied by the police rises to the level of "reasonableness."

---

[35] Plakas v. Drinski, 19 F.3d 1143, 48 (7th Cir. 1994) cert. denied 115 S.Ct. 81 (1994) ("There is, however, not a single precedent which holds that a governmental unit has a constitutional duty to supply particular forms of equipment to police officers"); Carswell v. Borough of Homestead, 381 F.3d 235 (3rd Cir. 2004) ("we have never recognized municipal liability for a constitutional violation because of failure to equip police officers with non-lethal weapons"); Salas v. Carpenter, 980 F.2d 299, 310 (5th Cir. 1992) (Constitution "does not mandate that law enforcement agencies maintain equipment useful in all foreseeable situations").

FOUR

The FBI and the Davidians at Waco in 1993

The next five chapters survey five representative (if peculiar) circumstances in which military and/or law enforcement authorities in different countries were called upon to apply various quantities of physical force against armed opponents. In each of these confrontations, violence erupted – many people died and much property was destroyed – and in each instance, reviewers have questioned the tactics, weaponry, and timing of the final assault, wondering whether some of the carnage might have been avoided. This chapter, and the four that follow, pick apart these incidents in some detail, focusing especially on the implements wielded by the opposing forces and raising the question of the possible utility of non-lethal weapons, especially the new and evolving NLW technologies introduced earlier. In each chapter, we first examine the background to the firefight, then describe the shooting itself, then inquire what difference modern non-lethal devices might have made.

A. BACKGROUND ON THE WACO CONFRONTATION

A tumultuous religious community – many labeled it a cult – settled ten miles outside Waco, Texas, in the 1930s. By 1987 these Branch Davidians (a radical offshoot of the Seventh Day Adventist Church, which emphatically denied any continuing connection) were led by the messianic Vernon Howell, who later changed his name to David Koresh. As the sect grew, and as Koresh's control over them became absolute and bizarre, they developed an apocalyptic theology, with Koresh prophesizing an imminent, fiery end to the world.[1] The Davidians established their sanctuary, known as Mount Carmel, in a series of ramshackle buildings on a seventy-seven-acre compound, home to more than one hundred men, women, and children from a variety of countries. Under Koresh's charismatic leadership, they also accumulated an impressive arsenal of $200,000 worth of weapons, explosives, and equipment in anticipation of a millennial eruption, including submachine guns, .50 caliber heavy machine guns, hand grenades and a grenade launcher, AK-47 assault rifles, Ruger and AR15/M16 semiautomatic rifles, Beretta semiautomatic pistols, quantities of explosive black powder, and night-vision goggles. Eventually the accretion of all this firepower – especially the illegal possession of automatic firearms, and the purchase of several kits to convert semiautomatic weapons into fully automatic capability – came to the attention of federal authorities. At the same time, reports (including from defecting members of the cult) about Koresh's frequent practice of child sexual abuse also aroused concern.

---

[1] The best sources regarding the Waco tragedy include Dick J. Reavis, *The Ashes of Waco: An Investigation* (1995); James R. Lewis (ed.), *From the Ashes: Making Sense of Waco* (1994); Brad Bailey and Bob Darden, *Mad Man in Waco* (1993); Clifford L. Linedecker, *Massacre at Waco, Texas* (1993); John C. Danforth, Final Report to the Deputy Attorney General Concerning the Mt. Carmel Confrontation at the Mt. Carmel Complex, Waco, Texas, November 8, 2000; U.S. Department of Justice, Report to the Deputy Attorney General on the Events at Waco, Texas, February 28 to April 19, 1993, redacted version, October 8, 1993 (hereinafter Report to the Deputy); Activities of Federal Law Enforcement Agencies toward the Branch Davidians, Joint Hearings before the Subcommittee on Crime of the Committee on the Judiciary and the Subcommittee on National Security, International Affairs, and Criminal Justice of the Committee on Government Reform and Oversight, U.S. House of Representatives, 104th Congress, 1st session, July 25, 26, and 27, 1995, Serial No. 72 (hereinafter Activities Toward).

After more than a year of investigation, approximately seventy-five agents and support personnel of the federal Bureau of Alcohol, Tobacco, and Firearms (ATF) entered the Mount Carmel compound on February 28, 1993, intending to serve an arrest warrant on Koresh and a search warrant for the illegal weaponry. Before they reached the front door, the Davidians abruptly opened a hailstorm of fire; fusillades of bullets were continuous in both directions for forty-five minutes and sporadic for eighty more – by some estimates, ten thousand rounds of ammunition were expended in the shootout. Four ATF agents were killed and sixteen others wounded in the ambush; inside the compound, there were five deaths and an unknown number injured, including Koresh. An uneasy truce was brokered, and the federal agents withdrew from Mount Carmel in shock. Shortly thereafter, the ATF requested the assistance of the Federal Bureau of Investigation (FBI), which then assumed leadership responsibility for future dealings with the Davidians. By midnight, more than three hundred law enforcement officers were on the scene.[2]

A fifty-one-day standoff ensued, with FBI negotiators engaged in sporadic, maddeningly frustrating telephone negotiations with Koresh and his subordinates. Over the first month, some thirty-five

---

[2] The issue of who fired the first shot is still disputed, and much of the evidence is equivocal or has long since disappeared. See Frontline, Waco: The Inside Story, www.pbs.org/wgbh/pages/frontline/waco/view (2002); Reavis, supra note 1, at 138–42; Activities Toward (Part 1), supra note 1, at 520–1, 632–3.

After-action analyses concluded that the ATF had lost the element of surprise; someone had tipped off the Davidians about the planned raid, and instead of arriving at a time when many of Koresh's men would be working outside the main building, unarmed, the law enforcement team arrived when the group was well prepared. In addition, federal agents were startled by the number and firepower of the Davidians' weapons, saying they were simply outgunned. Committee on the Judiciary, in conjunction with the Committee on Government Reform and Oversight, U.S. House of Representatives, Materials Relating to the Investigation into the Activities of Federal Law Enforcement Agencies toward the Branch Davidians, 104th Congress, 2nd session, Serial No. 12, August 1996, pp. 34–44 (hereinafter Materials Relating); Linedecker, supra note 1, at 166; Bailey and Darden, supra note 1, at 162–6.

people (twenty-one children and fourteen adults) were allowed by
Koresh to leave the compound. No shots were fired by either side
throughout the siege, but an array of law enforcement personnel
unprecedented in American history was assembled. On average, 217
FBI agents were present at the site each day, along with perhaps five-
hundred other officers from the ATF, Waco police, the McLennan
County Sheriff's office, the Texas Rangers, the U.S. Army, the Texas
National Guard, and other agencies.[3]

B. THE ASSAULT: APRIL 19, 1993

Determined to bring the standoff to a conclusion, the FBI assembled an assault force, medical teams, firefighting equipment, and a
variety of military and paramilitary vehicles, including five Combat
Engineering Vehicles (CEVs – M60 tanks with booms attached,
instead of gun barrels), two M1 Abrams tanks, nine M2AO Bradley
fighting vehicles, and two helicopters. At 5:55 A.M. on April 19, the
CEVs advanced into the compound, punching holes in the walls
of the Davidians' main building and inserting CS tear gas – liquid
streams covering approximately fifty feet in fifteen seconds – into
first-floor corner rooms. The original plan was to escalate gradually
the amount of CS dispensed, and to inject it into additional portions
of the buildings, incrementally contaminating the compound over
forty-eight hours, until the Davidians were flushed out. This action

---

[3] The military presence at Waco was substantial, but subordinate to law enforcement.
Under the 1878 Posse Comitatus Act, 18 U.S.C. 1385 and the Military Assistance to
Law Enforcement Act, 10 U.S.C. 371–8, the military is barred from performing direct
law enforcement functions (such as conducting arrests, searches, and seizures) inside
the United States, but can act in support of domestic civil authorities by providing
training, information, medical support, reconnaissance, equipment, maintenance, and
advice in extraordinary situations. That augmentation authority can be substantial,
in terms of both personnel and equipment. See Danforth, supra note 1, at 5, 33–46,
125–32, 138–40; Materials Relating, supra note 2, at 57–102.

was accompanied by oral messages, delivered via loudspeaker and telephone, assuring the Davidians that the FBI was not undertaking a comprehensive assault, and that people who wished to leave the compound could do so safely via passageways cleared through the three-foot high concertina wire barrier that surrounded the installation.[4] The Davidians, however, responded with a barrage of gunshots.

The law enforcement officers did not return this fire, but the CEVs and Bradley vehicles did bash down more sections of the compound's walls, and grenade launchers shot 389 Ferret rounds with more CS into the buildings. There followed a pause, with sputtering attempts at further negotiations and additional injections of CS. Shortly after noon, the climax occurred: simultaneous fires erupted in three or more locations inside the facility, and systematic gunfire from inside resumed. The flames, fanned by 30 mph prairie winds, reached nearly two thousand degrees Fahrenheit; they quickly engulfed the entire structure, and the flimsy Mount Carmel compound essentially burned to the ground inside forty-minutes. The remains of seventy-five people (fifty adults and twenty-five children), including Koresh, were recovered from the ruins, many of them bearing evidence of

---

4 Federal officials had debated whether Koresh and the Davidians were suicidal – the evidence, including statements from Koresh, other Davidians, and outside experts, was quite contradictory – and law enforcement leaders feared that an all-out assault might prompt the most extreme reactions. A more limited move, by gradually inserting tear gas and compelling the inhabitants to exit Mount Carmel, was thought to be less provocative. Edward S. G. Dennis, Jr., U.S. Department of Justice, Evaluation of the Handling of the Branch Davidian Stand-Off in Waco, Texas, February 28 to April 19, 1993, redacted version, October 8, 1993, pp. 6–8, 16, 22, 25–6, 36–9; Report to the Deputy, supra note 1, pp. 50, 210–14, 257; Michael Isikoff, Reno, FBI Took Fatal Gamble, Washington Post, April 21, 1993, p. A1. But see James D. Tabor, The Waco Tragedy: An Autobiographical Account of One Attempt to Avert Disaster, in Lewis, supra note 1, at 13 (concluding that Koresh would have surrendered peacefully if the standoff had continued only a little while longer); Timothy Lynch, No Confidence: An Unofficial Account of the Waco Incident, Cato Institute Policy Analysis No. 395, April 9, 2001.

having been shot at close range (presumably suicide or execution by other cult members during the fire). Nine Davidians somehow survived the conflagration.[5]

C. WHAT MIGHT HAVE BEEN

The FBI and the other law enforcement officers on the scene fired no shots during the April 19 tragedy or throughout the preceding fifty-one-day siege.[6] They were, of course, heavily armed, with an array of powerful tools now traditional for SWAT teams and a number of special accouterments for this occasion – and an assortment of NLWs as well. For example, "flash-bang" concussion grenades were available for use in any assault; the ATF had thrown some on February 28, and the FBI occasionally applied them during the siege to drive back indoors any Davidians who ventured outside into the yard. During the initial engagement, the ATF agents carried nonlethal fire extinguishers, to spray carbon dioxide at the Davidians' many dogs, deterring them from attacking. The concertina wire barrier, too, is a form of NLW, designed to ensure that the Davidians could not have escaped the blockade by shooting their way out of the compound – and equally to make certain that no outsiders could enter the facility to join Koresh as reinforcements.

Bright lights, loud noises, and raucous music, likewise, can be primitive NLWs. The FBI sought to wear down the Davidians'

---

[5] After the fire, investigators recovered 305 firearms from the compound, as well as 1.9 million rounds of ammunition that had been expended by the Davidians or been "cooked off" in the fire, and four hundred thousand rounds of live ammunition. Report to the Deputy, supra note 1, at 309–11; Danforth, supra note 1, p. 175.

[6] Some analysts concluded that the FBI did fire shots into the Davidians' compound during the April 19 climax, but careful (albeit, belated) technical analysis of videotapes of the incident failed to establish reliable evidence of such action. Danforth, supra note 1, at 5, 17–29; Lynch, supra note 4.

resistance by depriving them of sleep, through nightlong glaring stadium lights and exposing them to repeated playing of recordings of annoying sounds such as dental drills, seagull squawks, shrieks of rabbits being slaughtered, sirens, telephone busy signals, crying babies, trains in tunnels, and low-flying helicopters, as well as jarring music including Tibetan Buddhist chants, reveille, marches, Mitch Miller renditions of Christmas carols, selections from Alice Cooper, and Nancy Sinatra's 1960s pop ode "These Boots Were Made for Walking."[7]

A variety of critical factors impeded the FBI's application of conventional deadly force throughout the ordeal. There were children in the compound, as well as an unknown number of persons who might not be fully willing participants in Koresh's vision. The adults occasionally held children up at the windows, reminding the law enforcement officials of the danger of striking innocent victims. Also, the Davidians were armed with powerful, long-range lethal weaponry of their own, requiring a safety standoff zone that kept law enforcement personnel at a distance – enlarging the perimeter that had to be protected and patrolled, and requiring that fire fighting and medical

---

[7] At one point, Koresh responded in kind to the FBI's recordings, by setting his own (even larger) stereo speakers in the compound's windows and broadcasting loud rock and roll music back at the agents, in an all-night battle of the NLW bands. Frontline, Waco: The Inside Story, www.pbs.org/wgbh/pages/frontline/waco/view; John B. Alexander, *Future War: Non-Lethal Weapons in 21st Century Warfare* (1999), p. 47.

The FBI also shut off the electricity to the compound at irregular intervals, stopping Mount Carmel's lights and heat; the Davidians had only a limited capacity to produce their own electricity via generators. The FBI also controlled the telephone lines, allowing the Davidians only calls to and from the law enforcement negotiators. Except by turning off all the electricity, the FBI was not able to interdict the Davidians' access to television and radio; on one occasion, law enforcement officials worried that Koresh might have seen a provocative televised report that could have compromised their negotiating strategy.

After the Waco incident, FBI Director Louis J. Freeh issued a memorandum barring most forms of broadcasting of tapes of chants or other types of noises in future hostage negotiations. He concluded that such tactics "have no legitimate basis." Materials Relating, supra note 2, at 763.

staff and equipment also remain somewhat remote during the final assault.[8]

How should we evaluate the use of this, or any other, tear gas in this type of situation?[9] CS (actually an aerosol powder, rather than a true gas) is the leading lacrimator, causing temporary but acute and disabling irritation to the eyes, mouth, nose, and upper respiratory tract. It was invented by chemists B. B. Corson and R. W. Stoughton in 1928 and by the 1960s had established itself as the predominant riot control agent for use by police and the U.S. military (including extensive application in combat in Vietnam) and for personal protection by individuals. CS is less lethal and causes less long-term injury (particularly to the eyes) than any of its predecessors, but its overall safety was still in question – particularly when employed against children or pregnant women, and especially when used in confined spaces or for long durations, as contemplated at Waco.

The April 19 tear gassing came three months after the United States had signed the Chemical Weapons Convention, but the treaty had not yet been ratified, so it was not legally in force for the United States. In any event, this sort of operation would have been a valid application of a "riot control agent" for a "purpose not prohibited" under the convention, that is, "law enforcement."[10]

---

[8] One Davidian who left the compound had also warned law enforcement officials that Koresh planned a suicide bombing, by having a member of the cult strap explosives around his waist, to detonate when they surrendered to the FBI. Dennis, supra note 4, at 37; Activities Toward (Part 3), supra note 1, at 357 (prepared statement of Attorney General Janet Reno).

[9] Attorney General Janet Reno later recalled that, when assessing the FBI's proposed plan for inserting CS into Mount Carmel, "I said isn't there something that you could distribute through an airplane and just fly over and put them to sleep for an hour while we go in and get them out and was told that there was no technology that could be provided." Activities Toward (Part 3), supra note 1, at 362.

[10] Convention on the Prohibition of the Development, Production, Stockpiling and Use of Chemical Weapons and on Their Destruction, opened for signature January 13, 1993, S. Treaty Doc. 103–21, 1974 U.N.T.S. 3, 32 I.L.M. 800, entered into force April 29, 1997, art. II.7, 9; Activities Toward (Part 2), supra note 1, at 394, 428–9 (testimony

Could a more effective, safer chemical have disabled the Davidians quickly enough to pre empt their shooting at the FBI and enable an effective surprise assault? In particular, would a more deft delivery mechanism – not violently and repeatedly puncturing the walls of the main building – have quietly sedated or rousted the members, and not frightened them into believing Koresh's assertions that armageddon was neigh? What if powerful malodorants had been inserted into the building – would the people (especially the children) have been peacefully driven outdoors? Is it imaginable that biological means might have been able to befoul (or ruin the taste of) the Davidians' food and water supplies – a stockpile that the FBI feared might have enabled the cult members to hold out even through a yearlong siege?

Alternatively, could nonchemical means have addressed the situation? If acoustic rays could have penetrated the walls of the buildings and incapacitated the residents, would the Davidians have surrendered meekly? Could deployment of non-lethal barrier materials (e.g., slippery foam or sticky foam) have guaranteed that particular locations, such as the compound's water tower and watch tower, were effectively off-limits for the Davidians, ameliorating FBI concerns that such perches could have been occupied by snipers? When one of the .50 caliber guns was ominously propped into a window, could NLWs have somehow negated it in a nonexplosive fashion, thereby removing one of the worst threats, without Koresh's even realizing that his deterrent had been compromised? Could novel devices have rendered all the Mount Carmel windows opaque, so cult members could not effectively see (or shoot) out of them, thereby equalizing things with the FBI, which did not know what was going

of Hays Parks). See Chapter 3 for discussion of the legal requirements of the Chemical Weapons Convention.

on indoors and was instructed not to fire weapons into a room unless it was clear who was there?

Could snipers have used a long-range NLW to incapacitate, but not kill, Koresh when he appeared at a window of the compound, providing a moment for a sudden assault? Could modern electronic means have shut down the Davidians' access to radio and television (even if they had used their generators after the FBI turned off the compound's electricity), further isolating the cult, and ensuring that potentially damaging news broadcasts did not reach them? If an assault had become necessary, would it have been possible for the FBI to employ non-lethal projectiles, or perhaps electric stun guns, at least until they were confident that a particular room or wing of the building was not occupied by children – or by other members of their own squads?[11]

To ask these questions, of course, is not to answer them, either on the level of the tactics and tools that might be available today (or in the future) but were not in the inventory in 1993, or on the level of whether it would have been prudent to attempt them in this particular situation. But it does provide grist for speculation about how the increasing panoply of NLWs might enlarge the range of options that law enforcement officials could call upon in unyielding crises of this sort.

As discussed in Chapter 3, the operative legal standard for assessing a law enforcement use of physical coercive power is "reasonableness" – an elastic yardstick that requires case-by-case analysis, taking into account all the relevant circumstances. Notably, police are not required to use "the least possible" force or to escalate

---

[11] By some estimates, as many as half the casualties suffered by the ATF officers during the February 28 raid may have come from "friendly fire" – bullets shot by other law enforcement officers that accidentally hit their colleagues instead of the Davidians. Moorman Oliver, Jr., Killed by Semantics: Or Was It a Keystone Kop Kaleidoscope Kaper, in Lewis, supra note 1, at 71, 77.

their application of power only when lesser measures have proven unavailing.

Some outside observers charged that the ATF, FBI, and other units applied excessive, unreasonable power – they wanted to characterize federal agents as "jackbooted thugs" invading a peaceful, if bizarre, settlement. But a true measure of the legality of the operation must take into account the validity of the warrants to be served, the reasonableness of the belief that the Davidians were engaged in illegal operations, and, especially, their massive, heavy weaponry and the degree to which they had assiduously dug themselves into their fortification. The FBI demonstrated great patience throughout the lengthy siege, finally deciding to force a confrontation only out of frustration with the sputtering negotiations and dismay at the prospect of an indefinitely continued standoff.

Finally, it is noteworthy that U.S. courts reviewing a law enforcement use of weapons do not ordinarily second-guess the procurement decisions that created the available array of weapons at the authorities' disposal. That is, even if hindsight suggests that better chemicals or an improved array of other modern NLWs might have been effective, police are not liable for their much earlier failure to have purchased those devices. The legal judgment would inspect what the law enforcement officers on the scene in Waco might have done – not what additional array of possibilities could have served their purposes if different systems and technologies had been available to them.

In sum, the Waco confrontation was an unmitigated disaster from start to finish – among the least successful of our five case studies. The ATF and the FBI both failed utterly in their objectives: the main malfeasors were not arrested, the premises were not searched, the contraband was not seized. Instead, eighty-four people died; only forty-four of those who had originally been inside the Mount Carmel complex survived. February 28, 1993, was recorded as the bloodiest day in the history of the ATF, and one of the most costly days in all of American law enforcement; April 19, 1993, inflicted lasting damage upon the reputation of, and the public support for, federal authorities.

This is not the place to second-guess the original ATF incursion, the FBI's negotiation strategy during the fifty-one-day standoff, or the timing and planning of the tear gas operation. Our concern is with the weapons – lethal and non-lethal – employed, not with whether arms could have been avoided altogether by snatching Koresh when he was away from the compound, or by adopting a more low-key, nonconfrontational style. And it must be remembered that the primary blame for the gunplay, the inferno, and all those unnecessary deaths lies with David Koresh, the "sinful messiah" of Waco, who led his devoted flock to accumulate, and then to fire, the vast illegal arsenal and finally to torch their home, consigning themselves and their own children to horrifying deaths.

The intransigence of the Davidians (as well as their foresight in preparing for a lengthy standoff) created a most difficult and uncertain situation for law enforcement – all paths were risky, and even with 20/20 hindsight, it is difficult to discern any approach that would have guaranteed success. Federal authorities earnestly attempted to save lives – Attorney General Janet Reno's personal commitment to protecting children was well known – and FBI agents demonstrated incredible discipline and good judgment by not firing into the compound during the fifty-one days or during the April 19 denouement.

The law enforcement agencies did benefit from some basic NLWs – flash-bang grenades, obnoxious sound and light projections, simple barrier systems – but their available inventory was woefully inadequate for the task. Reno later reflected the obvious conclusion, saying that if she had known how the Davidians would respond to the tear gas injections, she would not have proceeded – but she really did not have many good alternative choices. Tear gas was just about the only available tool that offered much hope of peaceably flushing the cult members out of their encampment.[12]

In the aftermath of Waco, Reno undertook to expand the array of options for future incidents. She wrote a watershed request memorandum to the Secretary of Defense and secured agreement to expanded interdepartmental collaboration in the pursuit of advanced NLWs. The Department of Justice already had initiated a small research program in pursuit of non-lethals, but by teaming with the Pentagon and the Central Intelligence Agency, much greater progress could be achieved. Merging the frequent experience that local and federal law enforcement had garnered with simple NLWs, with the greater technology and resources of the national security community, could offer synergistic benefits to both sets of partners.

One other reflection on Waco: it provided a sampling of both the best and the worst environments for bringing NLWs to bear. On the one hand, the ATF had already been ambushed, losing four of their own to a barrage of deadly fire, and agents had concluded that part of the reason for the fiasco was being "outgunned" by superior firepower. That is surely a most inhospitable setting for application of non-lethal technology; a natural human instinct will be to exert maximum force, being your toughest, when already bloodied in battle.

On the other hand, the extended duration at Waco eased some of the logistical difficulties traditionally associated with NLWs. The fifty-one-day delay provided ample opportunity to marshal, prepare,

---

[12] Dennis, supra note 4, p. 63 (concluding that "Even if the FBI had been more keenly aware of [Koresh's] intentions, it was limited to gassing the compound as the only non-lethal means of resolving the crisis").

plan, and practice with the optimal munitions; the Mount Carmel site was a sitting duck, serviced by adequate roads, electric grid, and other supporting infrastructure. So this was not a situation where law enforcement officials had to choose between bringing to bear traditional lethal or novel non-lethal arms – both sets of equipment could be assembled at leisure. While in some other circumstances, police or military units may face a stark choice about what alternative pieces of equipment to carry with them into sudden battle and what tactics to employ in split-second decision making, it is worth noting that not all weapons applications play out at that rapid pace.

FIVE

The United Nations and the Rwandan Genocide in 1994

The second case study is of an altogether different sort. In Rwanda in 1994, the relevant confrontation presented a complex kluge of coup d'état, civil war, cross-border invasion, and ethnic genocide, with the competent outside forces – the United Nations, the United States, France, and Belgium – basically passive and ineffectual until the devastating internecine carnage had run its evil course. As in the other chapters, we present here (a) the background on the crisis, (b) a description of the climactic uses of deadly force, and (c) an appraisal of how things might have played out differently. But there is an important contrast with other chapters: in this case, there is little analysis of how the leading governments might have usefully restrained their application of familiar lethal weapons if non-lethal weapons had been available. Instead – in view of the fact that the outside forces were so feckless in doing virtually nothing to arrest the mindless slaughter – the remaining question is whether non-lethal capabilities *could* have helped inspire any quicker, more decisive foreign engagement. That is, we are reduced to asking whether the putative rescuers might have found modern NLWs helpful, if they had been otherwise motivated to inject themselves earlier into the bloody Rwandan turmoil?

A. BACKGROUND ON THE RWANDA CONFRONTATION

Rwanda is a small, very densely populated central African country – about the size of Vermont, with a population estimated at eight million in 1994. Formerly a colony of Germany, and then of Belgium, it attained independence in 1962 and has been persistently tumultuous ever since. The two main population groups (ethnographers resist labeling them as distinct races or tribes) are the Hutus (which constituted 85 percent of the population by the mid-1990s) and the Tutsis (making up approximately 14 percent of the population at that time).[1] The relationship between the two groups has always been complex and erratic. On the one hand, Hutus and Tutsis have regularly proven quite compatible: for centuries, they have spoken the same language, followed the same religions, and embraced the same customs. Hutus and Tutsis historically have lived and worked intermingled with each other, and they frequently intermarried. It is difficult, even for natives, to differentiate between the two based on physical appearance, speech inflection, or surnames (although Tutsis tend to be taller and lighter skinned, with straight noses and thin lips). Only the Rwandan national identification card, carried by all citizens, clearly identifies group affiliation.

On the other hand, Tutsis and Hutus have regularly attacked and killed each other in massive bloodbaths; as UN Secretary-General Boutros Boutros-Ghali noted, "Rwanda had endured seven large-scale massacres since 1959."[2] For example, Hutu extremists slaughtered between five thousand and eight thousand Tutsis

---

[1] But see Alan J. Kuperman, *The Limits of Humanitarian Intervention: Genocide in Rwanda*, 2001, pp. 19–20 (noting substantial uncertainty about the size and composition of Rwanda's pre-1994 population, suggesting that Tutsis constituted only about 8–9 percent of the country's population).

[2] United Nations, *The United Nations and Rwanda 1993–1996*, Blue Book Series Volume X, 1996, p. 37.

in 1963; another purge (triggered by a corresponding carnage of Hutus in neighboring Burundi) led to a major exodus of Tutsis from Rwanda in 1973. The antagonism between the two groups was exacerbated by the European colonial administrators, who somehow decided that the Tutsis were the superior group and entrenched them in positions of national leadership and control, establishing a dominance that survived into independence. Hutu resentment at this mistreatment seethed continuously and erupted occasionally.

Not coincidentally, Rwanda's larger neighbor to the south, Burundi, followed a similar path – hostility between the Hutus and the Tutsis infected both nations and provided an ample source of discord between them. Irredentist pressures perpetually regenerated themselves in both states, and ousted political and military figures obtained easy refuge in one country whenever they were out of power in the other.

In 1974 General Juvenal Habyarimana, a Hutu, then the Rwandan Minister of Defense, led a coup, overthrowing and killing the incumbent president. Habyarimana eventually transitioned into a civilian government, but he retained authoritarian control, juggling his prejudice against the Tutsi with a bias in favor of the northwestern region of the country, where he and many of his closest associates had originated. In response, exiled Tutsis, largely based in Uganda, formed the Rwanda Patriotic Front (RPF), which they molded into a most impressive political and military force.

In 1990 the RPF invaded Rwanda and achieved considerable tactical success, setting in motion a serpentine series of events: Habyarimana grudgingly agreed to open the political process to multiparty politics; a sequence of cease-fires was crafted, violated, and reinstituted; and massive displacement of civilians bred a continuous refugee crisis.

The watershed documents, the Arusha Peace Accords, defining the terms of a comprehensive, internationally supervised settlement between Habyarimana and the RPF, were signed in August 1993. Under this structure, the Rwandan constitutional apparatus would convert from a presidential into a parliamentary system of diffused powers; a transitional government would be created in which the RPF, Habyarimana, and other Hutu parties all shared control; and the Tutsi armed forces would be integrated into the national military pursuant to a formula that would require significant demobilization of Hutu fighters. The UN Security Council endorsed the Arusha Accords in October 1993, but Habyarimana dragged his feet and continuously obstructed their implementation. RPF forces were allowed to establish a battalion of six hundred troops in Kigali to provide security for the incoming Tutsi leadership, and another RPF battalion was stationed in northern Rwanda. These units were joined in late October by the first of twenty-five hundred soldiers from the UN Assistance Mission for Rwanda (UNAMIR), designated to assist in the implementation of the Accords, the monitoring of demilitarized zones, and the integration of the two armies.

Extremist Hutus, however, rejected the movement toward peace, and plotted against their former colleague Habyarimana, who was accused of the sin of creeping toward moderation. Democratization and demilitarization represented profound threats to these ruling elites, and the hardliners coalesced into militias – up to thirty thousand strong (virtually as large as the country's national army) – known as *Interahamwe* (meaning "those who work together") and *Impuzamugambi* ("those with a single purpose"). These and other vigilante groups harassed Tutsis and moderate Hutus, generated domestic turmoil in Kigali and throughout the country, and – most ominously – plotted the massive and sudden assassination of their opponents.

The triggering moment came at 8:30 P.M. on April 6, 1994. An airplane carrying Habyarimana and Cyprien Ntaryamira, the president of Burundi, was hit by a surface-to-air missile and crashed, killing everyone aboard, while on final approach to its scheduled landing at the Kigali airport. The two leaders were returning from a summit meeting of regional heads of state in Tanzania and had finally agreed to proceed with prompt implementation of the Arusha Accords. Although responsibility for the downing of their plane has never been unambiguously established, most observers conclude that it was ordered by irreconcilable Hutu extremists, led by Col. Theoneste Begosora. In short order – adhering to a well-constructed, comprehensive script – rampaging groups blamed Tutsis for downing the aircraft and used that pretext to undertake what soon became an astonishingly rapid and rapacious genocide.

B. THE ASSAULT: APRIL–JULY 1994

Within half an hour after the presidential plane had crashed, police, military, presidential guards, and the irregular militias erected selective roadblocks throughout the capital city and began hunting down their first, most prominent targets. Tutsis, as well as moderate Hutus who had supported reconciliation, were abruptly stopped, identified, and killed. The hostile forces had planned the bloodbath with excruciating skill; they conducted it with ruthless efficiency and speed. As Linda Kirschke wrote,

Within the first week, an estimated 20,000 people were killed in the Kigali area alone. In less than three months, approximately 500,000 were slaughtered; two million became refugees; and one million were internally displaced. French historian Gerard Prunier estimates that 80 per cent of the victims were killed during the first six weeks of the genocide, an extermination rate which would prove five times as fast as that of the Nazi death camps.[3]

Among the highest priorities on the extremists' hit lists were government officials who might be expected to resist their genocidal ambitions. Prime Minister Agathe Uwilingiyimana was immediately isolated, surrounded in her home, and assassinated; ten Belgian peacekeepers assigned to guard her were disarmed, taken prisoner, transported to a military base, tortured, and killed. The Minister of Agriculture, the Minister of Labor and Social Affairs, the Minister of Information, and the President of the Supreme Court were all killed, as per plan, as were scores of journalists, activists, intellectuals, priests, and human rights workers.

The carnage quickly spread to the countryside, leaving defenseless Tutsis no place to flee. The entire nation was caught up in the violence, as neighbor suddenly turned with insane viciousness against neighbor, robbing, raping, burning, murdering, and mutilating. The organized police, military, *Interahamwe*, and *Impuzamugambi* led the assault, but in many instances, ordinary people – Hutus who had previously demonstrated no particular hatred of Tutsis or any propensity toward violence – suddenly morphed into killers. There were precious few "innocent bystanders" – those who were not actively participating in the ethnic cleansing were presumed to be Tutsis or accommodationists, and suffered the same fate.[4]

---

[3] Linda Kirschke, Broadcasting Genocide: Censorship, Propaganda, and State-Sponsored Violence in Rwanda, 1990–1994, published by Article 19, October 1996, at 18 (citations omitted).

[4] Gerard Prunier, *The Rwanda Crisis*, 1995 ("The main agents of the genocide were the ordinary peasants themselves. This is a terrible statement to make, but it is unfortunately borne out by the majority of the survivors' stories"); Christian P. Scherrer, *Genocide and Crisis in Central Africa: Conflict Roots, Mass Violence, and Regional War*, 2002, p. 115 (positing "[t]he existence of probably over a million murderers").

One indispensable tool for organizing and spurring the genocide was the incitement provided by "hate radio." In a land where television was rare and newspapers episodic, a handful of widely accessible radio stations – particularly Radio Rwanda and Radio-Television Libre des Mille Collines – served a unique function, and the extremists utilized that mode with alacrity. Constant messages streamed across the airwaves decrying (real and imagined) past Tutsi outrages, warning of imminent RPF attacks, and rallying the citizenry to the murderous tasks. In the early days after the plane crash, radio broadcasts identified leading Tutsis by name, pointed out their locations, and called upon crowds to deal with them. Later, when the opposition had been effectively decapitated, broadcasters switched to a more generic anti-Tutsi harangue, incessantly urging the audience to undertake, and then to complete, a genocidal purge.[5]

Much of the killing proceeded via remarkably low-tech means. This was not a campaign of jet fighters, tanks, and heavy artillery; there were no mass Auschwitz-style gas chambers or crematoria. Instead, this was death via hand-to-hand combat, with amateur killers interacting face-to-face with their panicked victims. Untold numbers were dispatched by machetes, kitchen knives, or primitive clubs studded with nails; stoning was utilized in many cases.[6]

The defenseless Tutsis sometimes tried to fight back, but they, too, lacked modern weaponry or armament and were vastly outnumbered. In many areas, the frightened Tutsis sought refuge in central gathering places – schools, churches, sports stadiums, hospitals, and the like – huddling in groups of dozens, hundreds, or even thousands.

---

[5] See generally Kirschke, supra note 3.
[6] Alison Des Forges, Leave None to Tell the Story: Genocide in Rwanda, Human Rights Watch, 1999, p. 127 (from January 1993 through March 1994, Rwanda imported 581,000 machetes, enough for one-third of the adult male Hutu population; in addition, the only Rwandan manufacturer of machetes reported selling more in February 1994 than it had during the entire previous year.)

Initially, these communal facilities may have provided a measure of protection, as the attacking Hutu militia were held to a standoff by the defenders' makeshift fortifications. Soon, however, better-equipped Hutu armies, reservists, or national police would arrive, laden with rifles, grenades, or machine guns. They would lay siege to the site, set fires in it, and assault with their more powerful weaponry. Any Tutsis who attempted to flee would be inexorably cut down.[7]

Foreigners were largely immune from the attacks. Outside journalists, business people, human rights workers, and others who had remained in the country were very rarely harmed deliberately. In fact, in some instances, the mere presence of foreigners seemed to dissipate the violence; the Hutu militia was reluctant to allow outsiders to witness their activities and would slink to other locations, biding their time to renew an assault when the foreigners were no longer around.[8] In some horrific settings, UNAMIR, the Red Cross, or other international organizations tried to establish and monitor sanctuaries, extending a mantle of protection over as many people as they could, or transporting them to safer areas. In many instances, however, even these attempts proved ineffectual, as the extremists would remove selected Tutsis from the facility or camp each day for "interrogation" or under other false pretenses; the victims were never seen alive again.[9]

---

[7] Kirschke, supra note 3, at 130–1 (reporting massacres at churches).

[8] There were occasional, isolated attacks upon United Nations forces in Rwanda, in which disorganized crowds had to be dispersed by warning shots fired into the air. Des Forges, supra note 6, at 163, 598; Howard Adelman and Astri Suhrke (eds.), *The Path of a Genocide: The Rwanda Crisis from Uganda to Zaire*, 1999, p. 262.

[9] Jonathan C. Randal, Saved by French Troops, Rwandans Thank God: Tutsis Celebrate Mass under Guard, *Washington Post*, June 27, 1994, p. A1; Adelman and Suhrke, supra note 8, at 264–8 (noting several partially successful attempts by UNAMIR to protect local citizens, but concluding "it is also clear that the U.N. force had little capacity, and mostly assigned the lowest priority, to protect ordinary Rwandan civilians").

The RPF fought valiantly and successfully against the government army. The six-hundred-strong RPF battalion in Kigali and the corresponding unit in the northern Byumba prefecture both moved immediately to protect as many Tutsis as they could. Other, larger RPF forces quickly invaded from Uganda, fighting their way toward the capital. Despite remarkable military success, however, the campaign took precious time – and within the three months required for the RPF to rout the Hutu armies, hundreds of thousands perished. Throughout this period, outside forces were conspicuous by their absence and inactivity. The UNAMIR commander, General Romeo Dallaire of Canada, struggled with a contradictory mandate and a restrictive leadership at United Nations headquarters in New York. Even before the fateful plane crash, Dallaire had gotten wind of the genocidal plan; he had likewise learned of a depot where a cache of weapons was being held in readiness for that occasion – yet he was ordered not to intervene.[10] During the worst of the killing spree, UN forces were essentially confined to their quarters with restrictive "rules of engagement" authorizing the use of force in self-defense only. On the occasions when Dallaire himself would attempt to inspect the developments, Hutu officials delayed, misrouted, and hemmed him in, and he was precluded from reacting forcefully.

By the end of April 1994, the Belgian army contingent (the most competent unit under United Nations command) had precipitously withdrawn, and only 450 UN forces remained in Rwanda – and the

---

[10] On January 11, 1994, in what has become infamous as the "genocide fax," Dallaire reported an informant's warnings about the extremists' plot to provoke a civil war and to slaughter Tutsis. The informant also identified a depot of 135 weapons, which Dallaire proposed to capture immediately. Three days later, senior UN officials responded, ordering Dallaire not to conduct the raid and instructing him to query Habyarimana about the horrible plot. When he did so, that fact was quickly leaked to the hardline opposition. In February, UN officials finally did authorize Dallaire to assist the government in seizing weapons caches, but very few arms were ever captured.

Security Council was seriously contemplating a complete pullout. On May 17, however, Security Council resolution 918 zigzagged in the opposite direction, authorizing a surge to fifty-five hundred troops, under a renamed and reinvigorated UNAMIR II.[11] But few of those augmentation forces had actually arrived before the killing spree was complete, and their efforts to deliver aid or to protect victims were largely frustrated.

Individual foreign national military units were no more proactive than those of the United Nations. France, Belgium, Italy, and the United States each undertook successful "noncombatant evacuation operations," to extricate their nationals from Kigali at the outset of the fighting. But they offered no such escape hatch, or any other form of protection, to Rwandans. On more than one occasion, the departing foreigners, safe in the arms of their military rescuers, bid a tearful farewell to Tutsi friends and co-workers who were abandoned to an *Interahamwe* mob.[12]

In one particularly shameful incident, the American Department of Defense was requested to take action to shut down the most pernicious broadcasts of hate radio – either by jamming the transmissions or by disabling or destroying the facilities. The Pentagon brusquely responded that any such activity would be too expensive

---

[11] United Nations Security Council, S/RES/918, May 17, 1994. The Security Council imposed an embargo against shipments of war-related materials to Rwanda; expanded the UNAMIR mandate to include protecting displaced persons, establishing secure humanitarian areas, and supporting the distribution of relief supplies; and emphasized the permission for UNAMIR forces to take necessary actions in self-defense.

[12] French and Belgian citizens were evacuated from Kigali aboard military airplanes, while the U.S. Ambassador, David P. Rawson, determined that an overland truck convoy would be a safer means for extracting the approximately 250 Americans still in the country. Regardless of the means of transport, however, only the foreigners, not local citizens, were taken to safety in Burundi or elsewhere. Robert Pear, U.S. Envoy in Rwanda Decides on Overland Convoy to Evacuate Americans, *New York Times*, April 10, 1994, p. A6; Jennifer Parmelee, Americans Are Out of Rwanda; Rebel Army Advances on Bloodied Capital, *Washington Post*, April 11, 1994, p. A1.

and difficult. Certainly, any more ambitious intervention, to attempt to save the lives of countless Tutsis, was dismissed as impractical due to logistical difficulties.[13]

The interval between April (when Habyarimana's plane went down) and July (when the RPF's military success had essentially captured Kigali and most of the countryside, effectively ending the genocide) was certainly complex and confusing. Multiple disruptions were occurring simultaneously in Rwanda, and outside observers were understandably unable to follow events with insight and understanding. There had been, in short order, a murderous coup d'état, a full-scale war between the self-proclaimed successor Hutu government and the RPF invaders, and a brutal campaign of ethnic cleansing. Foreigners were quickly made aware of the chaos and bloodshed, but could not immediately grasp the enormity of what was happening. They heard reports of massive civilian deaths, but perhaps were muddled in differentiating between the "normal" collateral damage and refugee crises inherent in civil strife versus the absolutely abnormal genocide that was occurring without check.

Other factors, too, promoted footdragging and impeded efficacious foreign involvement. The United States, which only one year earlier had suffered a humiliating defeat in Somalia at the hands of indigenous warlords such as Mohammed Farah Aideed, was chary about engaging again in an African imbroglio. The emerging consensus in Washington was that American forces should not be deployed too quickly in these chaotic environments – we should intervene only when significant national interests were at stake, when there was a

---

[13] See Adelman and Suhrke, supra note 8, at 103 (reporting that the U.S. Department of Defense had estimated that it would cost nearly $4 million to jam the provocative radio broadcasts.)

clear plan for success and an exit strategy, and when sufficient forces and equipment could be committed to do the job properly. None of that seemed applicable in Rwanda.[14] Belgium, likewise, had no stomach for large-scale military intervention in its former colony. Begosora and the other plotters had cynically, but correctly, calculated that early casualties – such as the peremptory slaughter of the ten Belgians who had been assigned to protect the Rwandan prime minister – would impel Brussels toward an immediate withdrawal. France had greater reason to remain engaged – Paris had long supported Habyarimana, in part as a counterweight to the Anglophone Tutsis and Ugandans. But France, too, remained above the fray, at least until June 22, when it launched Operation Tourquoise, a belated effort by two thousand troops to establish a Safe Humanitarian Zone for internally displaced civilians in the southwest provinces of Rwanda, adjacent to Zaire.[15]

It is difficult, even with hindsight, to identify the reasons why these outside leaders sat on their hands in the midst of a genocide. Some of it was ignorance, or perhaps wishful thinking – a failure to recognize how bad conditions were in Rwanda. Some of it was a lack of self-confidence about their ability to intervene effectively; how quickly could a major rescue operation be mounted, and would the war and the killing have "run its course" before the foreign rescuers could arrive? Some of it was a desire not to take sides – the future of Rwanda, in the long term, would have to be decided by

[14] The new American attitude was codified in Presidential Decision Directive 25, issued just as the outbreak of violence in Rwanda demonstrated its limitations.
[15] The RPF did not accept this French intervention; Tutsis generally viewed France as attempting to prop up the remnants of Hutu rule, rather than functioning as a neutral, disinterested humanitarian referee. Kuperman, supra note 1, at 44–51; Jonathan C. Randal, Rebels Take Chief Cities in Rwanda: French Forces Declare Protection Zones after Capital, Butare Fall, *Washington Post*, July 5, 1994, p. A1; Marlise Simons, French Troops Enter Rwanda in Aid Mission, *New York Times*, June 24, 1994, p. A1.

the Rwandans themselves, and intervention to protect the Tutsis would inevitably be interpreted as an anti-Hutu preference. If UN, American, French, or other troops had to kill government soldiers and *Interahamwe* militia members to restore order, that action might impede any eventual domestic reconciliation. Some of it, undoubtedly, was sheer racism, a disregard for the horror in remote Africa, where there were no strategic or economic interests at stake; and some of the explanation for Western passivity was preoccupation with the concurrent crisis embroiling NATO in the disintegrating Yugoslavia.

When the RPF finally succeeded in creating a semblance of normalcy – the effective conclusion to the genocide and the civil war can be pinned to July 18 – the full scale of the horror finally emerged. We will never know exactly how many Tutsis and Hutus were buried in unmarked graves, washed into the Kagera River, or otherwise forgotten – a death toll of eight hundred thousand seems most plausible. Tearful apologies followed from Bill Clinton and others, marked by oaths never to let this sort of thing happen again.

Even a decade later, Rwanda has still only barely begun to come to terms with the spasm of killing; the triage of rebuilding the devastated society is only starting. The loss of perhaps three-quarters of the Tutsi population, the economic wastage of combat, the overwhelming floods of refugees, the communal psychic scars – all will linger for decades. The criminal prosecution for war crimes, genocide, and crimes against humanity – proceeding in desultory fashion in both domestic Rwandan courts and in a specialized tribunal established by the United Nations – provides only a hollow remedy.[16]

---

[16] See Alan Zarembo, Judgment Day, 294 *Harper's Magazine* No. 1763, April 1997, p. 68 (noting that nearly three years after the genocide, almost one hundred thousand genocide suspects still awaited trials in Rwanda).

C. WHAT MIGHT HAVE BEEN

The fundamental problem that prevented the United Nations, the United States, France, and others from achieving a more favorable outcome in the Rwanda confrontation was not a failure of weaponry. It was not inadequate military capability or insufficient precision in the lethal ordnance – those countries simply decided not to invest themselves in a timely rescue mission.

Still, it is worthwhile to speculate about what might have been accomplished, had the outside forces been sufficiently motivated to try. In particular, could a modern toolkit of non-lethal weapons have proven useful – and might some of those types of weapons have provided capabilities that could have reduced some of the inhibitions that constrained the foreigners in 1994?

Start with a most conspicuous example: the neutralization of hate radio. We now know that modern non-lethal mechanisms would allow American forces to impede the pernicious communications quickly and easily, disrupting the extremists' command and control network, and removing the most obvious mechanism for stirring up the populace and directing them toward the defenseless targets. This function could be accomplished electronically (aircraft known as Commando Solo could reliably jam the transmitters' frequencies, although considerable logistics support would be required to sustain these flights from distant bases). Alternatively, physical – but nonexplosive and nondestructive – means could be derived to knock the noxious facilities off the air temporarily. NLWs in this mode could allow the stations to resume broadcasting promptly, when the genocidal spike had passed, enabling them to assist in disseminating a postconflict message of peace and unity. Today this mission could be accomplished quite quickly and reliably, without necessitating a major on-the-ground presence of troops or a cataclysmic explosion.[17]

Next, non-lethal barrier systems could have been employed to impede *Interahamwe* and *Impuzamugambi* units from seeking out their prey. Just as those militia utilized roadblocks and checkpoints to detain Tutsis and delay their flight to safety, outside militaries could have employed caltrops, rigid foam barriers, entangling nets, and other devices to hem in the attackers and to close off selected routes. Certainly, it is reasonable to suppose that if today's technology had been available in Rwanda in 1994, individual sites – for example, the prime minister's home – could have been quickly and reliably secured, and in a nonprovocative fashion.

On a more ambitious scale, some of those same NLW implements might have succeeded in establishing reliable safe havens for larger clusters of Tutsis. With today's NLW arsenal, selected buildings or locations could be secured against assault – and any individuals who elected to challenge the perimeter could be further disrupted by slippery foam or multisensory flash-bang devices. Acoustic or millimeter wave systems might succeed in keeping even adventurous potential attackers at standoff distances. Some of those same technologies could have been applied to help protect the transportation of Tutsis and their sympathizers, to enable them to find and enter the safety zones before the extremists could attack. And all that could be accomplished without killing, without upping the ante on violence.

In a similar vein, those NLW barrier systems might have proven effective in self-defense of UNAMIR soldiers (if the crowds had been

---

[17] But see Kuperman, supra note 1, at 91–2 (arguing that knocking hate radio off the air in April 1994 would not have stanched the bloodshed, because by that point the Rwandan population was already polarized and the mobs were mobilized; other communications mechanisms could have substituted for radio in disseminating genocidal directions).

more bold in confronting and challenging them) or in defending Western installations (if the Hutu army, police, or other forces had chosen to attack embassies, troop barracks, or commercial establishments). In reality, the extremists largely ignored or avoided those potential international targets, instead concentrating their fury on their compatriots, but there had been some violent confrontations with UNAMIR early in the saga, and at least at the outset, no one could be confident that the militants would be self-deterred against attacking foreigners. Effective non-lethal mechanisms could have increased confidence that UN and foreign-nation forces and installations were defensible without inflicting unnecessary deaths and permanent injuries.[18]

A different array of barriers might have assisted in patrolling Rwanda's borders and airports, to interdict arms shipments and enforce the UN weapons embargo that had been declared in May. A landlocked country, Rwanda was difficult to resupply, and effective sanctions might have carried some impact (although the vast majority of the killing was accomplished through low-technology means already at hand or imported earlier.)[19]

NLWs might have assisted in accomplishing one immediate noteworthy objective: the seizure and disposal of the weapons depot that Dallaire had identified in April. Although this particular site contained only about 130 weapons, and neutralizing it would not have

---

[18] Adelman and Suhrke, supra note 8, at 255–6 (noting an incident in March 1994, during which a UNAMIR battalion fired on an unruly crowd, leading to a reprimand and instructions not to fire without authorization). Foreign installations were quite vulnerable during the crisis; by early April, U.S. forces had been withdrawn from Kigali to Burundi, and "there were no Marine guards and just a handful of United Nations peacekeepers at the American Embassy in Rwanda." Robert Pear, U.S. Envoy in Rwanda Decides on Overland Convoy to Evacuate Americans, *New York Times*, April 10, 1994, p. A6.
[19] The UN embargo did deter or interdict some shipments of weapons into Rwanda, but France provided the ruling regime at least a half dozen airlifted cargos of weapons in violation of the UN order, either directly from France or through Zaire. Kuperman, supra note 1, at 44–5; Des Forges, supra note 6, at 156–7, 652–3, 660–5.

had a major impact on the killing, decisive action (especially if it were accomplished in a non-lethal, and therefore less-provocative, fashion) might have created a useful precedent, leading to the recovery of other weapons stockpiles too. NLW could have aided in quickly securing the site and rendering the seized arms useless.

Finally, perhaps most vividly, NLW could have assisted in breaking up the crowds of militia and of ordinary Hutus who were, somehow, temporarily marshaled to the insane task of genocide. Whenever these mobs gathered, trouble was sure to follow – they would find Tutsis and continue the purge of the community – but a simple malodorant or a deft application of a vortex ring might have impelled them to disperse. Lightly armed, and prone to back down anyway in the presence of foreigners, these incipient killing forces might have been held in check by even a modest show of non-lethal force.

Many of these functions, to be sure, could also have been performed by conventional forces, armed with the customary array of lethal arms. And in some situations – when confronting the regular army or other opposition elements armed with automatic weapons, for example – the greater firepower might be essential. But non-lethal weapons can offer a unique array of capabilities, perhaps preferable in confrontations of this sort.

For example, when the opposing offensive force consists of disorganized civilians, carrying machetes and homemade clubs, it may seem like overkill for UN or U.S. soldiers to apply automatic weapons or machine guns. But doing nothing in such a situation may be unacceptable, too. This could be a situation where it is unnecessary to "defeat" the enemy in the traditional sense – perhaps it would suffice merely to frustrate or impede the opposing force, providing a temporary interruption in the rapid flow of events, allowing time for ordinary citizens to come to their senses, escape the intoxicating hold of the government's extremist propaganda, and restore order. If a non-lethal force could have deterred aggression or even held it in abeyance for a short time, perhaps that pause in the cycle of killing could have grown.

Non-lethal force could also abate the image that the United Nations or individual foreign countries were "taking sides" in the internal affairs of a country. If the existing ordinary weaponry required the interveners to kill Hutus to achieve an effect, those deaths would not be quickly forgotten. In contrast, if the only impact of the gunfire were blunt trauma, teary eyes, or temporary nausea, the animosity may not have been long-lasting. Many of the Hutus, after all, had been pressed into their evil service by a combination of peer pressure, coercion from militia, and fear for their own lives. Surely they bear a profound responsibility for their horrible misdeeds, but wouldn't it have been better for all concerned if their temporary insanity were reined in by non-lethal force, instead of adding still further to the death toll?[20]

Another potential advantage of NLWs is revealed by the particularly mad circumstances of Rwanda, where it was difficult for all protagonists to identify friend versus foe, to discern reliably who was Tutsi, who was Hutu, and who might hold what political opinions. That difficulty in discrimination is a formula for chaos, with the potential for unintended collateral damage to accidental victims and with tragic losses through "friendly fire" mistakenly aimed at colleagues. At the same time, it is also a formula for troops to hesitate before firing, when they are unsure who and where the target is – and

---

[20] Conversely, the failure of the United States, France, and other nations to take any effective action in Rwanda drove many Tutsis to conclude that the foreigners were "taking sides" in the war in support of the Hutu extremists. Even an attempt at feeble "neutrality" was interpreted as tacit support for the genocide, and the RPF grew suspicious of the impartiality of UN peacekeeping efforts. Julia Preston, 250,000 Flee Rwanda for Tanzania: Ethnic Warfare May Have Killed 200,000, U.N. Says, *Washington Post*, April 30, 1994, p. A1.

delays or inhibitions of that sort can prove lethal too. NLWs can help ameliorate those difficulties, since the consequences of a mistake are lower. If the costs of an error in judgment, identification, or timing are reduced through reliance upon beanbag munitions, tasers, and sticky foam, then it becomes much more reasonable to seize the moment with strong action. NLWs, in short, can free the soldiers to be more proactive, more bold in ambiguous situations. They can act promptly and sort out the situation at relative leisure.

Not all NLWs would be useful in all situations, of course, and it is difficult to calculate exactly which capabilities would have been most worthwhile in particular circumstances. For example, some of the worst excesses in Rwanda were perpetrated by people who were drunk or high on drugs; in many instances there seemed to be a daily cycle of substance abuse and murder. It is also known that some NLWs, such as CS tear gas or Mace, have proven less effective against individuals already impaired by liquor or drugs. Evidence suggests that pepper spray and tasers are more effective under those conditions – but those data are also controverted, so the optimal NLW array is still unclear.

It is also worth noting that all these additional NLW capabilities would have been brought to bear in Rwanda only at some cost. The equipment itself, of course, would carry a price tag, as would the task of training the disparate national troop contingents that constituted the UN force. (Some twenty-four countries participated in the operation, providing units of very different skills, equipment, and readiness.) The logistics task of transporting and maintaining an array of NLW devices also should not be underestimated. This confrontation unfolded in a remote location in landlocked central Africa, where the airport was not reliably serviceable and where the roads from neighboring countries were barely adequate for ordinary truck traffic. The United Nations met severe difficulty in equipping its forces with even the most basic standard equipment; ensuring access to anything more sophisticated would have been even more unlikely. If a significant outside force had been required, and if in addition to its traditional complement of combat supplies it were required to convey a supplemental NLW inventory too, the burden could have been overwhelming.[21]

In sum, the Rwandan confrontation is by far the worst of this book's five case studies, and one of the sorriest chapters in recent global affairs. The failure there was not due principally to an inadequacy in the weapon systems that could have been brought to bear by the United Nations, the United States, France, Belgium, or others. These actors each decided, for multiple other reasons, to avoid timely and significant intervention. Over a period of months, when even a relatively small show of determined force by outside nations would have made a difference to thousands or perhaps hundreds of thousands of Tutsi civilians, no weapons – lethal or non-lethal – were marshaled in their defense.[22]

Still, even here, there is a case to be made for NLWs. Effective barrier, combat, crowd-dispersal, and other mechanisms could have made a valuable contribution. They would have lowered the cost of intervention, making it easier for authorities in New York,

---

[21] See Kuperman, supra note 1, at 52–62 regarding the substantial problems in transporting large quantities of troops and equipment into Rwanda, lacking sufficient airports, roads, and sea access. See also United Nations, supra note 2, at 50–1 (obtaining and maintaining even basic military equipment for the UN force in Rwanda was difficult and resulted in delays).

[22] There is still contention regarding the effectiveness of early outside intervention in arresting the Rwandan genocide. General Dallaire and Scott Feil have argued that even a small foreign military contingent – five thousand good troops, timely deployed with an active UN mandate – could have prevented most of the killing. Scott R. Feil, Preventing Genocide: How the Early Use of Force Might Have Succeeded in Rwanda, Report to the Carnegie Commission on Preventing Deadly Conflict, April 1998. In contrast, Kuperman, supra note 1, concludes that the genocide occurred so quickly, the West learned the truth about it so late, and the logistical problems of any intervention were so substantial, that even a concerted outside effort would have come too late to save most of the victims.

Washington, Paris, and elsewhere to commit themselves to a rescue. They could have enabled the governments to protect more Tutsis without killing more Hutus, helping to freeze a most difficult situation before it descended further into ignominy. Non-lethal capabilities alone would not have prevented the tragedy of the Rwandan confrontation, but they could have assisted outside forces in abating and dampening the worst of the genocide.

SIX

The Peruvians and Tupac Amaru in Lima in 1996–1997

Our third case study presents a striking example of a violent national response to an extended terrorist hostage confrontation. In this instance, Peru was assaulted by one of the worst rampages of international terrorism, sited in a most delicate legal and political milieu, with the highest potential diplomatic stakes. Lima's police and military units eventually responded with deadly – and amazingly successful – force, providing us another occasion to speculate about whether an array of modern non-lethal weapons might have provided additional useful capabilities.

A. BACKGROUND ON THE LIMA CONFRONTATION

The dual scourge of terrorism and ruthless counterterrorism killed as many as thirty thousand Peruvians during the 1980s and 1990s, creating a climate of fear, uncertainty, and division across the country. The most prominent indigenous terrorist group, Shining Path (Sendero Luminoso), adopted a Maoist orientation, endeavoring to restructure the country along a peasant revolutionary model. A smaller Cuban-inspired group, *Movimiento Revolucionario Tupac Amaru* (MRTA) was founded in 1984, offering a competing Marxist-Leninist vision for ridding Peru of foreign and imperialist influences. MRTA probably never attracted more than one or two

thousand members; its armed struggle against the government consisted mostly of relatively small and episodic attention-getting enterprises, such as stealing food from a supermarket or a hijacked truck
and distributing it for free in poverty-stricken neighborhoods, or
temporarily seizing a foreign press office or a radio transmitter to
broadcast a revolutionary exhortation. In addition to those Robin
Hood tactics, MRTA also orchestrated a number of more deadly
bombings and kidnappings, assaulting banks, corporate buildings,
police stations, and embassies. In its most high-visibility undertaking, MRTA in 1995 undertook an abortive attack on the Peruvian
national Congress building.[1]

The Peruvian government long seemed hamstrung or ineffectual in combating these uprisings, but when Alberto Fujimori was
elected president in 1990, he came into office with a pledge of much
stronger, more concerted action against terrorism, and by 1992 he
had seized near-dictatorial power. Fujimori quickly asserted comprehensive authority in the security campaign and succeeded in killing
or arresting many of the leaders of both Tupac Amaru and Shining
Path, and confining the detainees in the most abysmal prison conditions. For a while, it seemed as though Fujimori's tough tactics had
succeeded in breaking the back of the resistance movements.

On December 17, 1996, however, the remnants of MRTA
undertook a most audacious counterstrike, under the code name
"Breaking the Silence." Fourteen heavily armed guerrillas, led by

---

[1] MRTA adopted the name Tupac Amaru to memorialize indigenous fighters in two distinct eras. The first Tupac Amaru was the last ruler of the Inca empire before the Spanish
conquered Peru. The second Tupac Amaru was an eighteenth-century Indian who led
a rebellion against the Spanish colonizers.

The MRTA first gained widespread international attention following the 1995
attempt to occupy Peru's Congress, especially when a young American journalist, Lori
Berenson, was charged as a collaborator. Berenson was convicted of treason by a special
Peruvian military court and sentenced to life in prison; the term was later reduced to
twenty years.

forty-three-year-old Nestor Cerpa Cartolini, the most senior MRTA officer still at large, targeted the official residence in Lima of Morihisa Aoki, Japan's ambassador to Peru. They attacked a well-attended gala diplomatic event being staged to commemorate the upcoming sixty-third birthday of Japanese Emperor Akihito. The terrorists had planned their assault well, including renting a property next door to the residence: some of the assault team entered the Japanese enclave by scaling the surrounding fifteen-foot-high concrete wall or tunneling under it; some used explosives to blow a hole in the fence; some had insinuated themselves among the party guests by posing as caterers and waiters serving luscious hors d'ouvres.

Following an intense forty-minute gun battle, the surprised and outmanned local police and security officers retreated, locking down the residence. There were no serious casualties during the initial assault, but when the dust had cleared, the MRTA terrorists held some five hundred distinguished hostages, including a Who's Who of ambassadors, foreign ministry officials, government leaders, business people, and other luminaries.

The terrorists quickly moved to secure their position, by scattering antipersonnel landmines and booby traps throughout the grounds and on the roof of the Japanese compound and by emplacing high explosives at key locations. They issued their demands (release of Tupac Amaru members from prisons; improved national policies to help the poor; safe passage to their home base in the jungles of central Peru; and payment of an unspecified "war tax"). Many of the hostages, including all of the women, were released within the first few days, and more trickled out over the ensuing weeks. The "high-value" hostages remained in custody, including Peru's foreign minister and agriculture minister, six justices from the national supreme court, five leading generals, senior ambassadors, representatives of Japanese corporations, national legislators, and

Fujimori's brother – an unhappy assemblage of seventy-two for the duration of the siege.² Eventually, both sides settled into an uneasy status quo, anticipating an extended hostage drama, with negotiations seeming to sputter only intermittently and without much real progress.

Heavily armed police and military officers patrolled the perimeter of the residence and endeavored to put pressure of various sorts on the terrorists. For example, the government cut electrical and water service to the facility (although it did allow the Red Cross to enter with food, water, and medical supplies to support the increasingly stressed hostages as sanitary conditions deteriorated). During the initial fighting, police had fired tear gas into the compound, but the terrorists had brought gas masks that muffled the effects. (The captives were not so equipped and did suffer.)

The prolonged crisis, of course, attracted massive press coverage in Lima, particularly among correspondents from Japan, and managing that media frenzy was also a substantial police responsibility. On December 31, when authorities were allowing small clusters of press photographers to set up their equipment to take pictures of the front door of the ambassador's residence, a Japanese television cameraman bolted from the prescribed group, ran up to the front door of the residence, knocked loudly on it, and was abruptly admitted. The rest of the pack of journalists quickly barged in too, and there followed an impromptu "press conference," providing MRTA officials an unrivaled opportunity to present their views to an eagerly waiting public. A week later, two more newsmen again circumvented the police security perimeter, scaling walls and scrambling over the

---

² Seven American diplomats were among those initially taken prisoner (the U.S. Ambassador, Dennis Jett, had left the party only shortly before the takeover). The Americans were quickly released, along with, it seemed, the hostages from other countries that had developed similar reputations for adopting tough attitudes about not negotiating with terrorists.

roofs of neighboring buildings to enter the compound and meet with the terrorists.

Fujimori pledged to seek a peaceful, negotiated resolution to the crisis – an outcome that Japan, in particular, earnestly favored – but he conceded little, and the negotiations seemed unproductive. Soon the government began contingency planning for another possibility: an assault on the compound. A central element in the rescue strategy would include digging a tunnel from the same neighboring property that the terrorists had commandeered, to burrow beneath the walls and into the ambassador's residence. The police also undertook a variety of "psychological operations" initiatives against the MRTA terrorists, including employment of NLWs such as blaring martial music and Creole songs at the residence at high volume through loudspeakers. This tactic – combined with provocative ploys such as ostentatiously and irregularly moving tanks and other heavy equipment back and forth along the perimeter, parading troops in formation, flying helicopters low over the scene, and firing shots into the air – served not only to disorient and intimidate the terrorists and deprive them of sleep, but also to mask the sounds of the digging. The terrorists, however, may have learned of the tunneling plan anyway, through uncensored media reports, which the police were unable to quarantine.

The terrorists' selection of a foreign embassy property in Lima as their target posed special problems. Japan was closely identified with Fujimori and his government; Tokyo was widely appreciated as a major foreign investor in Peru, but, the MRTA argued, it was also both a prominent symbol and a reality of external domination. Moreover, international law accords embassy properties a special status: normally an ambassador's residence would be immune from law enforcement activities of the host government, unless the ambassador consents – and in this instance, Japan was adamant in favor of a nonviolent resolution.[3] As the weeks stretched on, Fujimori engaged in close consultation with Japan (and with the United States and other Latin American countries as well) but declined to foreclose any of his options.

B. THE ASSAULT: APRIL 22, 1997

As the desultory negotiations began to offer only diminishing hope for a reasonable resolution, the Peruvian security apparatus accelerated its planning for forceful contingencies. Fujimori assembled a 140-person joint task force with components from the national police force and from the elite army, navy, and air force special operations units, many of whom previously had received training from American and other experts. Under the code name of "Operation Chavin de Hauntar,"[4] the forces constructed a plywood replica of the ambassador's residence at a secluded naval base on the island of Fronton and repeatedly practiced their assault techniques and timing. When talks essentially collapsed on March 12, over the terrorists' most basic demand – freedom for some four hundred of their imprisoned comrades – the rehearsals intensified, and the moment for action drew near.

Four months of stalemate had inexorably driven the MRTA crew to lower their guard, and the hostage takers eventually fell into a routine that the rescuers recognized and took full advantage of.[5]

---

[3] Regarding the inviolability of foreign embassies under international law, see American Law Institute, *Restatement of the Law, Foreign Relations Law of the United States* (3rd ed.), 1986, secs. 464, 466.

[4] Fujimori selected this name for the operation in recognition of an ancient pre-Incan civilization known as the Chavin, which occupied the Huantar region. When attacked, the Chavin concealed themselves from their enemies in tunnels under their temples.

[5] The Peruvian government obtained excellent intelligence about the location and activities of the hostages and the guards. The vital data were acquired from hidden microphones spirited into the residence, from more sophisticated external electronic

Almost daily at 3:00 P.M., the terrorists suspended other activity to play an indoor soccer game in the residence's first floor reception hall; most of the fourteen Tupac Amaru members participated, while others loosely kept guard over the hostages, most of whom were held on the second floor.

On April 22 at 3:17, Fujimori gave final authorization for the assault, and the underground commandos (some of whom, with incredible patience, had lain in wait in the warren of tunnels for as long as thirty-three hours) detonated a massive explosion directly under the reception hall/soccer pitch. Eight of the terrorists were instantly killed or incapacitated by the initial blast, and others were surely stunned or confused. Three assault teams immediately converged on the house, undertaking a sudden, powerful, and exquisitely coordinated operation. Within one minute of the explosion, the first rescuers had thrust into the building, quickly making their way toward the hostages – some of whom had been surreptitiously forewarned by clandestine radio signals, three minutes before, that the mission was imminent.

The terrorists were armed with automatic weapons, antitank guns, a rocket launcher, plastic explosives, and grenades. The government forces were similarly equipped with light automatic weapons and handguns, as well as armored vehicles and machine guns in the security cordon.

After 126 days of standoff, the fighting consumed only sixteen minutes. All fourteen MRTA members were killed; two soldiers were killed and nine wounded. Several of the seventy-two hostages were injured by gunfire or explosives, and one, Peruvian Supreme Court Justice Carlos Giusti, suffered a fatal heart attack after he was shot.

eavesdropping devices, from American CIA Twin Condor reconnaissance airplanes, and from covert communications with the hostages.

The Lima assault came as a surprise to officials in Japan, the United States, and elsewhere, none of whom had been forewarned. But they quickly rallied to Fujimori's support and commended Peru on the skill and success of the bold operation, labeling it a decisive blow in the struggle against international terrorism.

C. WHAT MIGHT HAVE BEEN

The Lima rescue operation was so spectacularly successful that it is hard to second-guess the timing, tactics, or weaponry and difficult to specify how even a modern array of NLWs could have procured any better result. Still, there are some questions that ought to be asked, and some suggestions to be offered.

First, law enforcement's manifest difficulty in securing the perimeter of the residence throughout the four-month standoff demands a better system. If renegade journalists could rush through the net and into the terrorists' lair, others might be able to accomplish that maneuver, too – and the dangers of reinforcements for the fourteen MRTA activists were too high. Non-lethal barrier systems – slippery foam to coat the sidewalks, pathways, and roofs, for example, or rigid foam obstructions that could seal the doors and windows – might have been valuable. Police would need to ensure, of course, that they could remove, negate, or circumvent those barriers quickly and easily during their April 22 assault – they would not want their own mobility to be impeded by newly installed impediments. But some NLWs could have sufficed for that dual task, sealing the building against unwanted intruders, while still leaving the police and military a free hand.

Next, to further isolate the terrorists, could Peru have employed NLW systems to interdict telephone, radio, television, short-wave, and other communications systems? The terrorists' access to news reports might have compromised the secrecy of the strike force's tunneling operation, or suggested to the terrorists when, and what sort of, an onslaught was forthcoming. Fortunately, even with incomplete operational security, the government was able to achieve decisive tactical surprise, but that good fortune cannot be guaranteed. Sophisticated electronic means are now available to preclude the easy communications into and out of such a facility – although it is another trick to find a way, as Peru somehow did, simultaneously to tip off the hostages to lay low when the rescuers invade.

Would there be any non-lethal way to flush the terrorists out of their fortification? Clearly, random or inexpert use of tear gas and of raucous music broadcasts had little effect – they merely annoyed the MRTA and weakened the hostages, without producing any positive movement. Perhaps more deft use of non-lethal calmatives (to induce sleep or passivity) or malodorants (to compel everyone to evacuate an inhospitable environment) would have been worth considering. Perhaps potions could have been crafted that would evade the protection offered by the MRTA gas masks. As elaborated in a later chapter, however, there is still no magic NLW chemical potion that could safely and reliably accomplish those objectives, and perhaps there never will be. Moreover, the dividing line between a police law enforcement incident and a military combat operation is obscure in situations like this, so the applicability of the 1993 Chemical Weapons Convention remains problematic.[6]

In any armed assault in a hostage situation, careful consideration must be given to the possible advantages of NLWs: in the chaos of a firefight, stray bullets can easily strike cowering hostages or friendly forces. Even with devices that enhance the soldiers' vision

---

[6] Peru signed the Chemical Weapons Convention on January 14, 1993, but the treaty did not enter into force until April 29, 1997, a week after the conclusion of events at the ambassador's residence. Regarding the legal constraints of this treaty, see Chapter 3; regarding the treaty's application in another volatile confrontation, see Chapter 7.

and communications, there can be much confusion and uncertainty that risk unintended casualties. Here we still do not know whether the several injured hostages and rescuers were hit by terrorists or by "friendly fire." Tasers, stun grenades, entangling net devices, rubber bullets, or other non-lethal tools might enable the assault force to strike quickly, with less fear of imperiling unintended targets – they might be able to move even faster if they have less reason to worry that they may be aiming at an inappropriate target. Where NLWs reduce the consequences of mistaken identity, it becomes more appropriate to shoot first and ask questions later.

Finally, one must wonder why it was deemed necessary in Lima to kill all fourteen MRTA activists; reportedly two of them shouted "We surrender" moments before being cut down. Non-lethal restraint systems might enable police and military to quickly confine or incapacitate their enemies, disarm them, and reliably prevent them from continuing to fight or trigger explosives – without necessarily killing them. Taking some of these terrorists prisoner also might have proven to be a gain for Peruvian intelligence, as well as for humanitarianism – interrogating them might have revealed future MRTA plans or other organizational secrets. Killing all fourteen may also unintentionally have made them into martyrs for their cause, possible rallying points for the organization's diminishing cadres. Essential to any alternative NLW project, of course, would be suitable mechanisms for ensuring that captured terrorists were physically unable to detonate any armaments, including even explosives strapped to their bodies – but such non-lethal bindings might be available today.

In sum, the Lima experience was remarkably successful – perhaps the best outcome achieved in any of our five case studies – and seventy-one hostages were freed from a most perilous situation. Still, the result was far from perfect: seventeen people died, and the ambassador's residence was thoroughly shot up. Even now, we do not have a complete picture of exactly what happened at each phase of the police/military assault, so all we can do is guess whether and how advanced NLWs might have facilitated an even more favorable result. But the evidence suggests that an even better, safer, cleaner rescue might have been obtained through improved capabilities.

Review of this remarkable confrontation also reveals another relevant consideration. Peruvian forces were not initially equipped to deal with such a swift, organized, and brazen terrorist act, especially one undertaken inside a foreign diplomatic building. And perhaps an economically developing country – even one with a history of internal terrorism – cannot be expected to sustain large, multipurpose counterterrorism cadres, capable of responding quickly and effectively to an unpredictably wide array of sudden attacks. But this episode suggests that at least occasionally, the action unfolds only slowly, over a period of weeks or even months – which can provide an opportunity to procure additional hardware, organize and train an appropriate force, and practice the new-found capabilities before pressing into action. Often, of course, there is no such luxury of time, but sometimes there is, and even if an important NLW capability is not available in-house, perhaps it can be acquired, borrowed, or developed in sufficient time.

Finally, the Lima experience also casts light on the relationship between police and military concepts in contemplating lethal and non-lethal possibilities. Any assault of this sort carries grave risk – if the rescuers had not been so lucky in decapitating the MRTA leadership with the soccer game explosion, there could have been many more casualties among both the assault force and the hostages.[7]

---

[7] Reportedly, in early planning for an assault against the MRTA, Peruvian military officials proposed to undertake the assault in the middle of the night, and they anticipated that 75 percent of the hostages, 95 percent of the guerrillas, and twenty of the com-

How much risk is acceptable – and does the degree of tolerable "collateral damage" vary, depending on whether the incident is characterized in military or police terms? As Frank A. Bolz, one of the founders of the New York City police department's hostage-negotiating team, commented after the success in Lima, "I would be very concerned if local law enforcement thought that this is the way it should be done. This was a political situation involving diplomats, diplomatic locations, international politics. This was a military operation, and in military operations, there are acceptable casualties. In local law enforcement, there are no acceptable casualty rates."[8]

---

mandos probably would die in the fighting. Calvin Sims, Peru Officials Admit to Plan for Commando Raid on Embassy, *New York Times*, February 17, 1997, p. A3.

[8] Quoted in Philip Shenon, Rescue in Peru: Strategies; Raid Stuck to the Rules, with a Few Twists, *New York Times*, April 24, 1997, p. A13.

SEVEN

The Russians and the Chechens in Moscow in 2002

The fourth of our five confrontations flashed without warning across the global consciousness in October 2002, as Russian officials suddenly confronted a most urgent hostage/barricade crisis in their nation's capital. Again, the book first presents the relevant background on the event, then describes its dramatic (and still not fully understood) climax, then speculates on the alternatives that better non-lethal weapons might have provided.

A. BACKGROUND ON THE MOSCOW CONFRONTATION

Chechnya is a small (seventeen thousand square kilometers) long-turbulent region in southern Russia, with a population of approximately one million. It declared its independence in 1991, but unlike other restive Caucasian breakaways, Chechnya was not recognized by other states, and, after a period of some disinterest and passivity, Russia forcefully resisted its secession. Boris Yeltsin sent troops to Chechnya in 1994 to attempt to quell the separatist movement, but this campaign – despite a crushing Red Army presence in the Chechen capital city of Grozny – resulted in a humiliating defeat for the Kremlin. When the demoralized Russian troops withdrew in 1996, Chechens formulated a government and elected their own president; under a peace plan negotiated with Moscow, a decision on Chechnya's final legal status was to be deferred for five years.

Soon, however, any semblance of law and order collapsed, and the country descended into a morass of religious extremism, terrorism, banditry, kidnapping, and corruption. A series of terrorist attacks on apartment buildings and other civilian locations in Moscow and other Russian cities was linked to Chechnya, and in 1999 Vladimir Putin led a second offensive against the chaotic breakaway region. This time Moscow succeeding in reasserting a shaky partial control, albeit at a price of eighty thousand Russian troops deployed in the country in support of a Kremlin-installed government. Widespread terrorist outrages continued – even after Putin grandly declared an end to the military phase of the operation – with frequent large-scale deadly incidents both in Chechnya and in Russia. After September 11, 2001, and when links appeared between the Chechen rebels and the al-Qaeda terrorist network, international pressure for restraint on Russia waned, and Putin further strengthened his resolve to resist sovereignty for the breakaway province.

On October 23, 2002, some eight hundred people (mostly Russians, but including perhaps seventy-five foreigners) were enjoying an evening performance of the popular romantic musical *Nord-Ost* at the Dubrovka Theater Center in southeast Moscow, only about three miles from the Kremlin walls. At about 9:00 P.M., early in the second act of the show, fifty masked, camouflaged, and heavily armed men and women, led by Movsar Barayev, one of the most fanatic Chechen terrorists, entered the theater, seized control, and locked down the three-story facility. The terrorists confined all their hostages – audience, cast, and crew – to seats in the auditorium, emplaced 250 pounds of explosives amid them, and threatened to kill everyone unless Russia ended its military campaign in Chechnya, withdrew its forces, and granted independence.[1]

Over the next couple of days, the terrorists released several hostages, but there was sporadic gunfire too, and negotiations with the Russian government and a variety of other interlocutors eventually stalled. Moscow authorities reluctantly concluded that a peaceful resolution was not forthcoming; the terrorists seemed fully content to play the role of martyrs – and maybe they even preferred that outcome. Many of the Chechens who were closely guarding the hostages kept grenades and plastic explosives strapped to their bodies, for quick, suicidal detonation in the event of a rescue attempt. Around 3:30 A.M. on October 26, more shots rang out from the theater; one hostage was killed and a couple more were wounded – and no one outside could determine whether the threatened wholesale slaughter of the innocents had begun.[2]

B. THE ASSAULT: OCTOBER 26, 2002

Around 5:15 A.M. on Saturday, October 26, Russian special forces executed their hastily drawn plan, beginning by pumping a still-unknown quantity of a still-undisclosed chemical narcotic gas through the Dubrovka Theater's ventilation system. Everyone

[1] The most useful contemporary reporting on the theater crisis was from the *New York Times*, the *Washington Post*, and the BBC. See generally David Chazan, BBC News, Chechen Rebel Divisions, October 26, 2002; BBC News, Q&A: The Chechen Conflict, October 29, 2002; BBC News, The Moscow Theatre Siege – Transcript, January 15, 2004 (hereinafter BBC Transcript); Christian Caryl, Death in Moscow: The Aftermath, 49 *New York Review of Books* No. 20, December 19, 2002, p. 58; Monterey Institute of International Studies, Chemical and Biological Weapons Nonproliferation Program, The Moscow Theater Hostage Crisis: Incapacitants and Chemical Warfare, November 4, 2002.

[2] The Chechens had announced various deadlines for the beginnings of the executions, including the early hours of October 26. However, the gunfire that morning was not actually the commencement of organized killings – instead, it was a response to one of the hostages who, apparently at the end of his patience, suddenly shouted something and started to run. The terrorists shot and killed him, also wounding two others. No one outside the theater, however, could determine the scope and meaning of those shots.

inside – terrorists and hostages alike – quickly became groggy, listless, and unconscious. A few of the terrorists, apparently, recognized what was happening, but even they did not have the time, or the residual mental and physical dexterity, to detonate the explosives before they succumbed. Some fifteen-to-thirty minutes of chemicals rendered everyone inside the theater immobile, but some of the terrorists who were positioned in hallways adjacent to the theater auditorium remained unaffected.

By 6:00 A.M., two hundred of the Russian elite *spetsnaz* forces then launched their assault, barging into the theater from multiple directions by breaking down a wall, plunging through the ceiling, and bursting up from the basement. There was a short but intense firefight with some of the terrorists who had lingered in the foyer and on the second floor landing behind the balcony, unaffected by the gas. Grenades and small arms quickly suppressed this resistance, and the commandos then raced to locate the unconscious terrorists inside the theater; they immediately shot and killed them all.[3]

The troops next began defusing the terrorists' explosives, escorting or pulling hostages out of the building, and engaging medical personnel at the scene and across the city. Some 450 emergency teams were already on standby, and ambulances and even ordinary city buses were lined up to transport those in need of medical care. However, the Russian authorities had not advised the medics to be prepared for chemical casualties, as well as gunshot or explosion wounds, and in the chaos of the moment, emergency triage

---

[3] When the assault began, all the male terrorists immediately left the theater auditorium and prepared to engage in the gun battle against the attacking Russians; the female terrorists remained inside the auditorium with the hostages. In the end, the males were killed in the shootout with the *spetsanz* in the hallways; the females were then summarily executed while they were comatose in the theater. One officer explained the point-blank killing of the unconscious terrorists, "We were finishing off those who had explosives on them because people could come to or, on the contrary, convulsions could start." Michael Wines, Hostage Drama in Moscow: The Aftermath; Hostage Toll in Russia over 100; Nearly All Deaths Linked to Gas, *New York Times*, October 28, 2002, p. A1.

procedures sputtered. Doctors did not have enough of the key anti-dote, naloxone, did not know how much to administer, and – inexplicably – were not even told the exact nature of the sedative they were struggling to counteract. This failure – a failure that continues to date – to disclose precisely what drug the assaulting troops employed certainly impeded effective treatment of the patients and subsequent evaluation of the exercise.

In the end, the death toll for the assault included all fifty terrorists (killed by firearms) and 129 hostages (all but one or two killed by the narcotic gas). None of the assaulting *spetsnaz* troops were hurt in the fighting, but nine were injured by the effects of the chemical. Almost all of the surviving hostages were hospitalized after the rescue; many required treatment because of the gas for an extended period and may have incurred permanent disabilities. Supporters of the Russian government's decision claim – with good basis – that in the absence of forceful action, the terrorists most probably would have murdered all eight hundred hostages, and perhaps quite soon. Critics argue that the use of the still-mysterious knockout gas may have been premature; that the chemical was too powerful, killing 15 percent of the people it was intended to save; and that Moscow's possession and use of the substance in this situation may have violated its obligations under international law.[4]

C. WHAT MIGHT HAVE BEEN

The obvious "what if" question in this incident is to speculate about any possible alternative riot control or calmative chemicals that

---

[4] Uncertainty persists about the numbers of people involved in this incident. During the chaos preceding and following the assault, some of the hostages may have wandered off without being identified and accounted for; some terrorists, too, may have slipped away. There is no exact count, therefore, of the number and identities of those confined inside the theater during the crisis. BBC Transcript, supra note 1; Caryl, supra note 1; Nick Paton Walsh, *Families Claim Death Toll from Gas in Moscow Siege Kept Secret*, *Guardian* (London), October 18, 2003.

might have sufficiently disarmed the terrorists without killing so many of their hostages. More generally, could other tactics and tools of assault, including advanced NLW, have accomplished the mission with the requisite speed and power to retake the Dubrovka Theater safely without the use of chemical agents at all?

Russian authorities belatedly announced that the chemical pumped into the theater was based on a substance known as fentanyl, but they provided no further specifics. Outsiders have speculated that the sedative may have been the derivatives carfentanil, sufentanil, or remifentanil, or perhaps a chemical cocktail combining several such ingredients. Fentanyl is a well-known, potent, manmade opiate, utilized with frequency as a quick-acting, short-duration anesthetic in the operating room – but it is typically administered precisely, and only in concert with other drugs, because it can dangerously suppress respiration. Sufentanil is ten times stronger than fentanyl; carfentanil is ten times more powerful still. Carfentanil is not approved for human use, but is administered by veterinarians to tranquilize large mammals such as bison for treatment.[5]

Fentanyl, sufentanil, and carfentanil are not chemical weapons, like mustard gas or nerve agent. They are not listed on the schedules of the most tightly controlled toxic substances in the Chemical

---

[5] Michael Wines, The Aftermath in Moscow: Post-mortem in Moscow; Russia Names Drug in Raid, Defending Use, *New York Times,* October 31, 2002, p. A1; Paul Wax, Charles E. Becker, and Steven C. Curry, Unexpected "Gas" Casualties in Moscow: A Medical Toxicology Perspective, 41 *Annals of Emergency Medicine* No. 5, May 2003, p. 700 (noting that the Russian spokesman asserted that fentanyl "cannot by itself be called lethal"); BBC Transcript, supra note 1 (sufentanil is basically fentanyl with sulphur added; carfentanil is fentanyl augmented by carbon; the greater power of these derivatives means that a smaller quantity would have to be administered to have the desired effect; ordinary fentanyl could not have been pumped through the theater's ventilation system with the necessary speed); Monterey Institute, supra note 1; Bob Van Damme, Moscow Theater Siege: A Deadly Gamble That Nearly Paid Off, 269 *Pharmaceutical Journal* (7224), November 16, 2002, p. 723; David Brown and Peter Baker, Moscow Gas Likely a Potent Narcotic: Drug Normally Used to Subdue Big Game, *Washington Post,* November 9, 2002, p. A12 (carfentanil is eight thousand times as powerful as morphine).

Weapons Convention. They might fit the treaty's criteria for "riot control agents," in being characterized by rapid onset and short duration of incapacitating effects. Apparently, however, Russia has never registered any of these chemicals with the CWC's implementing organization under the treaty.[6]

The leading measure of a drug's safety and effectiveness in these types of applications is its "relative safety index" (or "therapeutic index") – the ratio of its "lethal dose" (or LD_{50} – the dose that would prove fatal for 50 percent of the people who receive it) to its "effective dose" (the ED_{50} – the rate that would have the desired therapeutic or sedating effect on half the treated individuals). In general, the greater the index, the safer the drug. For fentanyl, the relative safety index is approximately 277, meaning that a deadly dose is 277 times greater than the amount that should accomplish the intended sedating effect. For carfentanil, a much safer pharmaceutical in this sense, the index is approximately 10,000.[7]

Those statistics, however, are valid only for rigidly controlled applications, such as a hospital operating room, where the status (age, health, body mass, etc.) of the patient is well known and the

---

[6] See Chaper 3 regarding the legal obligations of the Chemical Weapons Convention. See also David Ruppe, CWC: Experts Differ on Whether Russian Hostage Rescue Violated Treaty, Global Security Newswire, October 30, 2002 (fentanyl was not declared by any country as a riot control agent under the requirements of the Chemical Weapons Convention); Monterey Institute, supra note 1. But note that the CWC reporting requirement on its face applies to chemicals used for riot control purposes, not to those intended for other types of law enforcement applications. Convention on the Prohibition of the Development, Production, Stockpiling and Use of Chemical Weapons and on Their Destruction, opened for signature January 13, 1993, S. Treaty Doc. 103–21, 1974 U.N.T.S. 3, 32 I.L.M. 800, entered into force April 29, 1997, art. III.1(e).

[7] Monterey Institute, supra note 1; Wax et al., supra note 5 (providing slightly different index values). Notably, if the objective is to incapacitate *everyone*, instead of merely 50 percent of the population (e.g., all the terrorists in a hostage situation), then much higher levels of the medication must be provided, with a correspondingly greater danger of overmedication. Sharon Liebetreu, The Moscow Dubrovka Theater Center Hostage Crisis: Chemical Incapacitants and International Law, unpublished seminar paper, Georgetown University Law Center, May 9, 2003, on file with author.

amount of the drug that is administered can be carefully modulated. In the Dubrovka Theater, however, exactly the opposite conditions prevailed: the people who inhaled the chemical were of vastly differing and unknown health profiles, and all were surely in decline, due to stress, enforced inactivity, and the absence of adequate food and water for fifty-six hours. They were located at quite different places throughout the theater – closer or farther from the building's air conditioning vents – meaning that they must have inhaled radically different amounts of the narcotic. They were unattended immediately after the exposure to the drug, so when they became unconscious, some slumped into awkward positions that constricted their airways, further reducing respiration. And after exposure, they were not afforded prompt treatment – and whatever palliative care they did receive was compromised by the Russian government's refusal to specify what chemical had been inflicted.

The sorry excuse proffered by the Moscow authorities – that many of the fatalities among the hostages had succumbed due to heart attacks, prior poor health, stress, and other complications – may contain a grain of truth, but the chemical, and the Soviet-style secrecy that still surrounds it, obscure valid conclusions.

Could a better chemical have been employed? There is, despite persistent research in Russia, the United States, and elsewhere, no magic chemical bullet. There is – and perhaps there never will be – a calmative gas that can rapidly and surreptitiously sedate or incapacitate a group of people distributed throughout a building, without killing some of them. No matter how great the hypothetical safety index, the danger of unintended casualties in these idiosyncratic, uncontrollable circumstances will always remain.

Opaque legal questions, too, surround the application of chemicals in this context. Was this truly a use of chemicals for treaty-permitted "law enforcement" against terrorists, or was it more akin to a prohibited "method of warfare" against armed rebels? The Chemical Weapons Convention does not define the borderline between those two forms of violence, and the corpus of international law likewise has trouble separating those sometimes-conjoined twins. The scale and frequency of the fighting surrounding Chechen separatism may seem sufficient to classify the struggle as an "armed conflict," at least for some purposes of international law, and the disparate locations of the plague of guerrilla violence – not confined to Grozny or Chechnya alone, but spreading to Moscow and other Russian cities – likewise seem to implicate a characterization nearing civil war.[8]

If this confrontation is judged by the standards of armed conflict, then the CWC would prohibit the application of any toxic chemicals (lethal or non-lethal) as a method of warfare. Even if Moscow officials believed in good faith that the fentanyl saved lives, and even if they were correct in that judgment, the world has turned its back on chemical combat, and some other mechanism would have to be found. In addition, the customary international law of

---

[8] Brandt Ahrens, Note, Chechnya and the Right of Self-determination, 42 *Columbia Journal of Transnational Law* 575 (2004); "Law Enforcement" and the CWC (editorial), 58 *Chemical and Biological Weapons Conventions Bulletin,* December 2002, p. 1; Ruppe, supra note 6.

Under the 1977 Protocol II Additional to the 1949 Geneva Conventions, the rules for "non-international armed conflicts" apply to fighting involving "dissident armed forces or other organized armed groups which, under responsible command, exercise such control over a part of its territory as to enable them to carry out sustained and concerted military operations" but not to "situations of internal disturbances and tensions, such as riots, isolated and sporadic acts of violence and other acts of a similar nature." Protocol Additional (No. II) to the Geneva Conventions of August 12, 1949, and Relating to the Protection of Victims of Non-International Armed Conflicts, June 8, 1977, 1125 U.N.T.S. 609 (United States is not a party), art. 1, paras. 1 and 2. See also Paola Gaeta, The Armed Conflict in Chechnya before the Russian Constitutional Court, 7 *European Journal of International Law* No. 4, 1996, pp. 563, 68 (Russian Constitutional Court has determined that the conflict in Chechnya is a civil war under Protocol II, as a prolonged internal conflict having great intensity). Of course, a "law enforcement" operation could occur even in the midst of an "internal armed conflict," so even if there were greater clarity about the legal characterization of the overall Chechen conflict, that would not by itself resolve the question of Russia's compliance with the CWC in the Moscow theater incident.

armed combat would bring to bear the requirements for avoiding "unnecessary suffering," for "discriminating" between combatants and civilians, and for refraining from attacking fighters who had already been wounded or otherwise rendered unable to resist. Alternatively, if this were judged to be a law enforcement operation, instead of combat, the legality under the CWC is still dubious. One might like to look more closely at the Russian chemical inventory itself: what, exactly, was this substance or combination of pharmaceuticals? Could it have been, as some have speculated, an entirely new member of the remarkable fentanyl family, unknown in the West? What quantities of the drug have been produced – and has Russia ever considered reporting it under CWC article III.1 (e)? Has it ever been used elsewhere? (There have been occasional murky reports of other applications of unknown chemicals in domestic riot control operations in the former Soviet Union.) How quickly do the disabling physical symptoms of the drug disappear (many hostages required extensive hospitalization and may suffer years of lingering effects), and how would it fit inside the CWC's definition of legitimate riot control agents as those that lose their effect "within a short time following termination of exposure"?[9]

Moreover, we would like to know more about the administrative side: which entity or entities within the Russian bureaucracy are responsible for this drug? Was it created for, held by, and applied by "military" forces (making it look more like a tool of war) or "police" forces (making it appear more akin to antiterrorism and domestic law enforcement)? The *spetsnaz* "Alpha Team" that conducted the assault on the theater is a hybrid commando unit of the Federal Security Service (FSB, the successor to the KGB); there were also plenty of local police and other law enforcement teams engaged

---

[9] Chemical Weapons Convention, supra note 6, art. II.7.

in the operation – all of which creates an additional film of legal ambiguity.[10]

NLW proponents also would question whether other, nonchemical assault tactics might have ameliorated the situation. Instead of (or in addition to) pumping some form of fentanyl into the theater, what if other non-lethal tools had been available? Could an effective acoustic system have penetrated the walls of the theater and suddenly incapacitated the terrorists; could a millimeter wave device, such as the Active Denial System, have immobilized them quickly enough to preclude their detonation of their explosives? One suspects that even vastly improved "flash-bangs," intended to stun the targets by sudden bursts of dazzling light and sound, would have been insufficient here – even with only a few seconds' notice, well-trained, disciplined, and committed terrorists might have triggered their doomsday devices. Likewise, even powerful malodorants might not have driven the Chechens out of the theater without their carrying out their threats. In any event, after the *spetsnaz* found the unconscious terrorists inside the theater, why did they peremptorily execute them, instead of immobilizing them with sticky foam, modern plastic handcuffs, or other secure, easy-to-apply non-lethal restraint systems, disarming them, and taking them prisoner?

In sum, the Moscow confrontation is still difficult to assess. The surreptitious injection of a supposedly non-lethal knockout gas killed over 125 hostages and seriously injured scores more of the very people it was supposed to help rescue. On the other hand,

---

[10] BBC News, Spetsnaz: Russia's Elite Force, October 28, 2002 (noting that the 1,500–2,000-man antiterrorist Alpha unit has seen extensive action in Afghanistan and Chechnya); BBC News, Gas "Killed Moscow Hostages," October 27, 2002 (quoting Lev Fyodorov, president of Russia's Union for Chemical Safety, as claiming that "This was a military operation using non-lethal chemical weapons developed during the cold war. . . . They would have been intended for a military opponent").

some seven hundred Russians and others survived their encounter with a most brutal terrorist – a far better outcome than most people would have predicted on October 25, 2002. The theater building was damaged by the assault and the shootout, but none of the terrorists' 250 pounds of explosives detonated, precluding a much wider swath of destruction. All of the terrorists, but none of the *spetsnaz* troops, perished.

Both Russian President Vladimir Putin and U.S. Ambassador to Russia Alexander Vershbow pronounced the raid a qualified success – but only when judged by the most desperate criteria, comparing the outcome to the complete disaster that could have eventuated. And both governments rightly assigned the real culpability for the disaster to Barayev and the scourge of terrorism.

Some of the fatalities surely could have been avoided, if not for the dark Soviet propensity for secrecy. Even if legitimate concerns for operational security might have inhibited informing medical teams in advance about what tactics the special forces would employ, there was no valid reason to refuse to disclose, after the assault, exactly what chemicals had been used, in what concentrations, and what antidotes might prove most availing. And the continuing secrecy over hospitalizations, morgue activities, and private lawsuits only fuels conspiracy theories and impedes intelligent "after action" analysis of lessons learned. Shooting the unconscious terrorists where they lay, instead of disarming them and taking them prisoner, also reflects a most troubling tactical choice – and perhaps an underappreciation for modern NLW tools that could immobilize and render harmless even desperadoes who had strapped explosives to their own bodies.

Given the fanaticism of the Chechens, it may have been impossible to negotiate a peaceful outcome – nothing short of precipitous Russian capitulation would likely have ameliorated the crisis. But this scenario is obviously not something that could happen only in Russia: hostage/barricade situations of varying scale are all too common around the world these days, inspired by terrorism, organized crime, domestic disputes, and drug impairments. In the same vein, future confrontations of this sort also may echo the Moscow experience by engaging, in some fashion, both the military special forces and the domestic law enforcement apparatus – it is still not clear how well the Dubrovka Theater incident fits into the neat dichotomies of military versus law enforcement and international versus internal. Nor is it yet clear how well Moscow's behavior, both before and during the confrontation, complied with the obligations of international law under the Chemical Weapons Convention.

The hope that technology – especially modern biochemistry – can provide a better solution to these tragedies-in-the-making is equally widespread. In these agonizing scenarios, we earnestly wish for some magic calmative potion that would instantly, safely, and totally incapacitate the combatants, enabling a lightning strike that could free the hostages, defuse the explosives, seize the firearms, and incarcerate the malefactors. But that sort of anesthetic pixie dust is currently unavailable – and may never be achievable. Although it is always risky to venture that something could never be invented, even with concerted R&D enterprise, Elisa Harris may have it right, at least for now, when she asserts, "The whole idea of nonlethal chemical warfare agents is a myth. Anyone who tries to suggest otherwise is ignoring the evidence."[11]

---

[11] Guy Gugliotta, U.S. Finds Hurdles in Search for Nonlethal Gas, *Washington Post*, November 1, 2002, p. A30 (quoting Elisa Harris, former Clinton Administration National Security Council official).

EIGHT

The British and the Iraqis in Basra in 2003

Finally, we turn for our fifth case study to an instance of conventional military combat. Or *nearly* conventional combat – when modern troops are engaged in "military operations in urban terrain" (MOUT), many of the ordinary verities of warfare are suspended or modified. The wrestling in Iraq at the outset of Gulf War II revealed many of the characteristic difficulties of fighting in an environment in which armed enemy troops are intermingled with civilians and with irregular, nonuniformed – but deadly – opponents, and in which the troops' assigned mission may creep inexorably forward.

A. BACKGROUND ON THE BASRA CONFRONTATION

Basra is an ancient city, Iraq's second largest, situated in the southeastern corner of the country, at the confluence of the historic Tigris and Eurprates rivers. It commands Iraq's only port (on the Persian Gulf), and its population (variously estimated as between one and two million) is squeezed between Kuwait to the south, Iran to the east, and the rich Rumeila oil fields to the west. Importantly, 60 percent of the residents are Shia Moslems, the sect that is numerically more common in Iraq, but that had for decades been repressed by Saddam Hussein and his predominantly northern Sunni Moslem brethren. Basra has therefore long been viewed with suspicion, at best, by Baghdad, and the city was rightly considered a possible source of smoldering antiregime sentiment.

In the run-up to the 2003 invasion, the United States, the United Kingdom, and their coalition partners fashioned a battle strategy emphasizing speed and flexibility, as well as overpowering force, with the intention of stampeding into the capital as quickly as possible and deposing Saddam Hussein. An immediate objective in that progression was to pounce on Basra; the Americans would quickly dispatch any organized resistance in the area, then advance north toward Baghdad, leaving to the British the tasks of quelling any lingering pockets of resistance in the south and occupying Basra. The expectation was that an immediate show of overwhelming force (the "shock and awe" campaign), coupled with local antipathy to the regime, might lead to a prompt negotiated surrender of Basra within only a day or two, obviating the need for prolonged localized fighting. Basra then could become a shining illustration of Iraqis' anti-Saddam fervor; of the Westerners being greeted as liberators, rather than resisted as foreign invaders; and of the benefits a city could obtain through enlightened, cooperative occupation.

Basra was defended by a surprisingly small force, consisting of perhaps only one to two thousand fighters, including remnants of the 51st Mechanized Division, armed with second-class equipment, such as outmoded Soviet-era T55 tanks. These less-than-frontline troops were supplemented by a few hundred *fedayeen*, the irregular militia of poorly trained but ruthless and fanatic devotees of Saddam Hussein and his Ba'ath Party. In command of the city was the notorious Ali Hassan al-Majid, a cousin of the dictator, who had earned the nickname "Chemical Ali" because of his brutal 1988 campaign, featuring illegal use of chemical weapons, against the rebellious Kurds in the northern part of the country.

A. BACKGROUND ON THE BASRA CONFRONTATION

The coalition's initial concept of operations called for the British to advance to, but not quite into, Basra; there the forces would pause, anticipating a surrender of the city, perhaps to be spurred by a spontaneous, indigenous Shia uprising against their longtime repressors. At all costs, the invaders wanted to avoid the specter of prolonged street fighting in Basra: the laborious process of a house-by-house campaign against the *fedayeen* would be both costly in terms of British soldiers' lives, and devastating to the process of building support from the Iraqis. If their city were turned into a battleground – even if it were a battle the coalition was confident about winning – the residents surely would despise an army that succeeded in "liberating" them only at the cost of destroying their homes and businesses and killing innocent civilians.

The first phases of the war went basically according to plan: the ground invasion began on March 20, 2003, and within about twenty-four hours, the United States and United Kingdom forces had traversed the twenty miles from the Kuwaiti border to the outskirts of Basra. It took a little longer than expected to suppress resistance in some of the small border towns on the Faw Peninsula, and to clear the harbor at Umm Qasr of mines, but British troops soon had Basra essentially surrounded, and the enemy forces inside it were bottled up.[1]

---

[1] Victor Mallet, Mark Nicholson, and Mark Odell, Attack on Basra Begins with Land and Sea Assault, *Financial Times* (London), March 21, 2003, p. 4; Patrick E. Tyler, A Nation at War: The Attack; U.S. Bombs Ravage Targets in Baghdad; Waves of Troops Sweeping South Iraq, *New York Times*, March 22, 2003, p. A1; Rajiv Chandrasekaran and Peter Baker, Troops Advance Halfway to Baghdad: Others Close in on Second-Largest City, *Washington Post*, March 23, 2003, p. A1; Oliver Burkeman, War in the Gulf: Basra: Battle for City Leads to "Massacre of Children" Claim: Allies Silent on Claim of Dozens Killed by Bombing, *Guardian* (London), March 24, 2003, p. 4; Richard Norton-Taylor and Rory McCarthy, War in the Gulf: British Plan to Take Basra by Force: Commanders Consider Whether to Move into City to Take Advantage of Reported Uprising, *Guardian* (London), March 26, 2003, p. 4.

The first consequence of battles near Basra was a humanitarian crisis. The city's electricity supply faltered, including a shutdown of power to critical water treatment facilities, leaving 60 percent of the residents without safe drinking water and nearly everyone without lights. Food and medicine did not seem to be in short supply, but UN Secretary General Koffi Annan warned that a health catastrophe was brewing in the besieged metropolis.[2]

With the British reluctant to jump into the city or to engage in large-scale artillery or airborne strikes against it, the defenders adopted a variety of tactics of "asymmetric" warfare, employing guerrilla, terrorist, and patently illegal maneuvers. They colocated military and civilian sites – placing tanks in residential neighborhoods, military headquarters next to schools, and armed troops at hospitals. They frequently abandoned the distinctive military or even paramilitary garb, dressing and fighting as civilians. There were suicide bombers, some of whom were coerced into that action by *fedayeen* threats against their families. There were fake surrenders, amounting to perfidy under the laws of armed conflict. The *fedayeen* used civilians as unwilling shields, grabbing children as cover to preclude return fire from the British. The defending forces also savagely repressed any dissent inside Basra, peremptorily executing resisters and those suspected of collaborating with the invaders; even refugees who sought to flee the imperiled city were attacked with small arms and artillery. In one instance, the *fedayeen* arrested, interrogated, and assassinated a leading local Shi'ite cleric whose loyalty to the regime was in doubt.[3]

---

[2] BBC News, Basra Faces Water Supply Crisis, March 23, 2003; Marc Santora, A Nation at War: Helping Iraqis; Continued Fighting Delays Plans for Aid Distribution, Relief Workers Say, *New York Times*, March 25, 2003, p. B6; Marc Santora, A Nation at War: Southern Iraq; Food Arrives, but Water Supplies Cause Worry, *New York Times*, March 27, 2003, p. B11.

[3] Patrick E. Tyler, A Nation at War: The Attack; Allies outside Biggest Southern City, *New York Times*, March 23, 2003, p. A1; Rory McCarthy, Richard Norton-Taylor

The coalition forces outside the city did call in some targeted bombings – one of which, with incredible precision, destroyed the Basra headquarters of the Ba'ath Party, while preserving basically unharmed a neighboring school on one side of the building and a hospital on the other. The strikes also destroyed a television tower that the regime had used to broadcast anti-Western propaganda to the population, some bridges over the region's waterways, the telephone exchange, and electrical facilities. The British also undertook occasional "smash and grab" raids to seize particular Ba'ath officials, and they established checkpoints on the major roadways, to inspect refugees who fled the city, but basically did not interdict the flow of unarmed individuals exiting or entering.[4]

An odd stalemate then ensued. Some twenty-five thousand coalition troops controlled vast areas of the southern countryside and neighboring desert, but few of the urban areas, and no part of Basra. The southern oil fields were protected – they were taken so quickly that the retreating Iraqis had no opportunity to set more than a few wells on fire, compared to the massive torching they had done in Kuwait in the 1991 Gulf War. The port was beginning to operate, and some imported humanitarian assistance was becoming available, but could only trickle in to the urban people in greatest need. There were some surrenders by disaffected or demoralized Iraqi

and Julian Borger, War in the Gulf: Troops Lay Siege to Basra, *Guardian* (London), March 26, 2003, p. 1; Richard Norton-Taylor and Rory McCarthy, War in the Gulf: British Plan to Take Basra by Force: Commanders Consider Whether to Move into City to Take Advantage of Reported Uprising, *Guardian* (London), March 26, 2003, p. 4; Patrick E. Tyler, A Nation at War: The Attack; Airstrikes Continue as Allies Consider Timing of a Thrust, *New York Times*, March 29, 2003, p. A1; David Ignatius, Hussein's Enforcers at Work, *Washington Post*, March 29, 2003, p. A17; Jeanette Oldham, Basra's Last-Stand Militia Using Five-Year-Olds as Human Shields, *The Scotsman*, April 2, 2003.

4 Keith B. Richburg, Basra Defenders Burrow into Residential Areas, *Washington Post*, March 24, 2003, p. A1; Nicholas Watt, War in the Gulf: Capture in Basra: Marines Hold Brigadier General as Residents Continue to Leave City, *Guardian* (London), March 31, 2003, p. 7; John F. Burns, A Nation at War: Baghdad; Iraqi General Says 4,000 Volunteered for Suicide Attacks, *New York Times*, March 31, 2003, p. A1.

troops, including one rather substantial group of the 51st Division at the outset of the fighting, which seemed to augur a repeat of the massive surrenders that had occurred in 1991, but overall, the Iraqi troops fought better, and surrendered less often, than anticipated.[5] Most distressing to the British was the apparent absence of any large-scale popular uprising against Saddam's regime. Fragmentary reports suggested that the residents were, indeed, eager to throw off their oppressors, and stronger reports of looting and lawlessness in the city revealed that the local authorities had lost substantial control of the situation. But the Westerners had, in hindsight, overlooked a crucial factor: the paralyzing fear that Saddam's minions had imposed on Basra. Even the slightest expression of dissent inspired ruthless retribution; as long as the most proximate authority figures were the *fedayeen*, they continued to command obedience.[6]

For two weeks the stalemate persisted, with the British perched just outside the city, incrementally tightening their grip, and the defenders still entrenched within. The British sometimes crept closer, and their airstrikes and artillery firing sometimes had an impact – on March 28, for example, accurate intelligence directed American F15E bombers to a building where the *fedayeen* were meeting, and two hundred fighters were killed. On April 5, prompted by another tip, British aircraft battered the home of "Chemical Ali." Early reports suggested that the despot had been killed, but that

[5] Victor Mallet, Mark Nicholson, and Mark Odell, Attack on Basra Begins with Land and Sea Assault, *Financial Times* (London), March 21, 2003, p. 4; Victor Mallet, Mark Nicholson, Mark Odell, and Peter Spiegel, Division of 8,000 Iraqi Troops Surrenders: Battle for Basra, *Financial Times* (U.K.), March 22, 2003; BBC News, Patient British Hopes for Basra, April 1, 2003.

[6] Keith B. Richburg, British Forces Confronted by Guerrilla Tactics, *Washington Post*, March 25, 2003, p. A1; Marc Santora, A Nation at War: Opposition Groups; Fear Said to Be Keeping Iraqi Dissidents from Rebelling, *New York Times*, March 26, 2003, p. B3; Roula Khalaf, Victor Mallet, and Mark Nicholson, Allies Admit Predicament as Basra "Uprising" Evaporates, *Financial Times* (London), March 27, 2003, p. 3.

turned out to be erroneous; still, it was an important psychological victory, underscoring the new vulnerability of even the top Ba'ath leadership.[7]

Most notably, the British undertook occasional probing raids into the city, with a group of tanks and other armored vehicles suddenly dashing toward the center, zipping down Basra's main corridors, engaging in brief firefights, and then withdrawing. With these tactics, the British were able to demonstrate that the defenders no longer exerted total control over Basra, to gather information about concentrations of enemy units (to provide targets for subsequent air and artillery fire), to destroy at least a handful of Iraqi tanks and other military equipment, and – by ostentatiously pulling down statues of Saddam and other symbols of the regime – to wage a "psychological operations" campaign against the *fedayeen* and in support of opposing civilians.[8]

For their part, the Iraqi fighters attempted to lure the U.K. forces into close-quarters street fighting. They would appear in small groups at the fringes of the city and take potshots at British encampments with rocket-propelled grenades or other portable equipment, hoping that the foreigners would pursue them into alleys and be ambushed. The British, however, steadfastly refused to be drawn into the city – they stressed that a major assault in the urban terrain would be disastrous for soldiers and civilians alike, and they clung to the hope that, eventually, that intense combat, and the inevitable collateral harm to residents' lives and property, would not be necessary.

---

[7] BBC News, "Saddam Loyalists" Bombed, March 29, 2003; Michael R. Gordon, A Nation at War: Military Analysis; Basra Offers a Lesson on Taking Baghdad, *New York Times*, April 7, 2003, p. B1.
[8] BBC News, Troops Relish Basra Statue Raid, March 30, 2003; Keith B. Richburg, Standoff at Basra Hints at Tough Time in Baghdad, *Washington Post*, March 30, 2003, p. A22; Tim Butcher, War in the Gulf: Marines: Commandos Launch Battle for Basra, *Guardian* (London), March 31, 2003, p. 7.

Occasionally groups of Iraqi vehicles attempted an abortive counterattack – a breakout from Basra, massing for an excursion to the south – such as a group of seventy tanks and other vehicles on March 26. But those columns were quickly obliterated by British fire, with such certainty that observers speculated that only something malicious such as *fedayeen* threats against the Iraqi soldiers' families could have impelled them into such a suicidal mission.[9]

As the standoff continued, Basra seemed to become, not the hoped-for symbol of an easy victory, prompted by local welcoming of coalition liberators, but precisely the opposite: an illustration of Westerners getting "bogged down" in the Middle East, stumbling into a tougher-than-anticipated military campaign, with only sparse indigenous support. The Westerners were not inflicting casualties upon the Basra residents, but they were being blamed for the slow pace of humanitarian relief, and for being overly cautious in dislodging the *fedayeen*. If it takes two weeks or more, instead of only a day or two, to capture Basra, what could be anticipated as the Americans and British tackled the presumably even less hospitable conditions in Baghdad?

B. THE ASSAULT: APRIL 6, 2003

The episodic British incursions into central Basra became more frequent and prolonged, and the troops also began to inch in from the periphery, establishing a camp just inside a key bridge over the Shatt al Basra waterway. On Sunday, April 6, U.K. forces undertook yet another of these in-and-out bursts, this one code named

---

[9] Keith B. Richburg and Susan B. Glasser, Iraqi Tanks Try to Break Out of Basra: British Troops Bombard City, *Washington Post*, March 27, 2003, p. A23.

Operation Sinbad (because the legendary Sinbad of 1001 Nights fame had been from Basra). On this occasion, two convoys (each comprising twenty-eight tanks, twenty-eight other armed vehicles, and fifteen hundred soldiers) followed separate routes into the heart of the city, converging at the College of Literature. To their surprise, they encountered significantly less resistance than usual, and on the spur of the moment, they decided to stay, rather than to beat the customary hasty retreat to the relative safety of the suburbs. A substantial British force of ten thousand then quickly followed the incursion, occupying critical portions of the city.[10]

A day of intense, but sporadic and disorganized, fighting ensued. Pockets of hostile fire were uncovered around the city, but the dwindling Iraqi forces were vastly overmatched. Only three U.K. soldiers were killed; perhaps three hundred Iraqi fighters died. There were very few surrenders by Iraqis – the remaining regular army and militia personnel either fought to the bitter end or, more often, doffed their uniforms and quietly slipped away, leaving Basra and melting into the countryside.[11]

When it became clear that the British forces were there to stay, and that the hated Ba'athists had at last been deposed, the local population reacted with enthusiasm. The residents welcomed the Westerners (at least to the point of expressing gratitude for their

---

[10] Michael R. Gordon, A Nation at War: Military Analysis; Basra Offers a Lesson on Taking Baghdad, *New York Times*, April 7, 2003, p. B1; Craig S. Smith, A Nation at War: In the Field, Basra; British Assault Captures Half of City in South, *New York Times*, April 7, 2003, p. A1; Peter Beaumont and Martin Bentham, War in the Gulf: After Two Weeks Kept at Bay, British Troops Cut Swath through Saddam Loyalists: Taking Basra: Dramatic End to Long Standoff at Party HQ, *Guardian* (London), April 7, 2003, p. 3; David Williams, The City Fell and Its People Cheered: Iraqis Throng the Streets in Celebration as Basra Is Liberated by British after a Day of Desperate Fighting, *Daily Mail* (U.K.), April 7, 2003.

[11] BBC News, "Large Parts" of Basra under UK Control, April 6, 2003; Keith B. Richburg, British Forces Enter Basra as Residents Loot City, *Washington Post*, April 7, 2003, p. A1; Williams, supra note 10.

assistance, leavened with suspicion about their true long-term objectives), and eagerly identified for them any hidden resistance fighters or weapons caches to be attacked or confiscated. The locals also violently took matters into their own hands against individual antagonists – lynch mobs attacked remaining police, Ba'athists, and others, settling old scores with revenge beatings and vigilante killings.

Most vivid was the looting. Years of pent-up frustration, coupled with the sudden power vacuum created by the Ba'athist collapse, created conditions for a looting rampage of incredible depth and vigor. Government buildings were stripped bare; other public facilities, such as universities, utilities, hospitals, and the like, were similarly shorn of furniture, vehicles, carpeting, appliances, and fixtures – anything that could be pried loose was expropriated. Even privately held property, with no connection to Saddam's regime, such as hotels and individual homes, became targets for the outburst of thievery. Garbage trucks, ambulances, and fire engines were all promptly stolen.[12]

The looting persisted even in the midst of the ongoing gun battles between U.K. troops and the remaining *fedayeen*. Within only two or three days, most of Basra was relatively secure, but some sections, such as the historic old city, where the streets were often too narrow for tanks to maneuver, remained in dispute. The British suddenly found themselves called upon to play a variety of incompatible roles: they were fighting a conventional war, they were engaged in sporadic urban antiguerrilla operations, and they were also asked

---

[12] Marc Santora, A Nation at War: The South; The Tides of Revenge in Basra Rise Quickly, *New York Times*, April 11, 2003, p. B2; BBC News, UK Troops Urged to Police Basra, April 8, 2003; BBC News, UK Aim to Restore Basra Order, April 8, 2003; Nicholas D. Kristof, A World Upside Down, *New York Times*, April 11, 2003, p. A25.

to provide a wide range of law enforcement, civil administration, and humanitarian functions.[13]

The U.K. forces temporized on the last of those responsibilities – declining to turn their attention to "governance" tasks, so long as active combat was still being waged (and, to some extent, not resisting the inclination of many Basra residents to vent their hostility by looting official buildings associated with Saddam). But residents demanded immediate British leadership in quelling the onslaught of looting and street crime – despite modest disarmament efforts, the city was awash in firearms, and no one felt safe. Even Saddam, for all his oppression, had enforced a measure of physical security for the residents – would their British liberators do less?[14]

As the fighting dwindled, and as the smoke cleared, it became apparent that the city of Basra had indeed been spared the worst ravages of urban warfare – there were plenty of damaged buildings, bombed bridges, and torn-up roads, but much of the critical infrastructure remained intact (or, at least, in no worse shape than it had fallen into during Saddam's reign). Many people were angered at the horrible individual misfortunes of war – bombs that had gone astray or that had accidentally taken their loved ones or their homes – and at the slow pace of refugee assistance. But there were not nearly as many grieving mourners as there would have been following a major

---

[13] Keith B. Richburg, Lawlessness Spreads in Villages: As Bandits Rove, Allied Forces Are Blamed for Not Enforcing Order, *Washington Post*, March 29, 2003, p. A1; Keith B. Richburg, British Troops' Dual Role: Soldiers and Relief Workers; Near Basra, Forces Hand Out Food, Water as Fighting Continues, *Washington Post*, April 4, 2003, p. A29; Keith B. Richburg, In Basra, Growing Resentment, Little Aid: Casualties Stoke Hostility over British Presence, *Washington Post*, April 9, 2003, p. A23.

[14] BBC News, UK Troops Urged to Police Basra, April 8, 2003; BBC News, UK Aim to Restore Basra Order, April 8, 2003; Richburg, supra note 13; BBC News, British Take on Balancing Act in Basra, April 8, 2003; Nicholas Watt and Richard Norton-Taylor, War in the Gulf: Security: Alarm as Lawlessness Goes Unchecked: Britain to Send Just Two MoD Police to Advise Troops as UN Leads Criticism of Coalition over Collapse of Public Order, *Guardian* (London), April 11, 2003, p. 4.

urban assault. Humanitarian aid – trucks distributing potable water and engineers attempting to restore the electricity grid, running water, and other public services – only very gradually came online.[15]

C. WHAT MIGHT HAVE BEEN

The question to ponder from this case study is whether advanced non-lethal weapons could have helped empower the British to have their cake and eat it, too – could there have been a mechanism that would have enabled them both to avoid the perils of street-by-street fighting, and to come sooner to the assistance of the beleaguered residents of Basra?

Perhaps the answer is no – the fundamental inadequacy of the situation was the difficulty in separating *fedayeen* and other hostile (but often covert) forces from the civilians, and where the residents are too terrified to provide the necessary intelligence and identification, there may be little that improved weaponry alone can add to the mix. But for some functions, current or projected NLW enhancements could have served a useful role.

The dilemma of dealing with human shields, for example, might have been ameliorated in some situations if the British had been able, via acoustic or other technologies, to disable everyone within range; the incapacitated then could be safely sorted out at leisure. Likewise, potential suicide bombers (those who volunteered for the horrific duty, as well as those coerced into it) might be identified and frozen by netting at standoff distances, permitting inspection

---

[15] Marc Santora, A Nation at War: In the Field, Basra; British Soldiers' Long Battle for a Southern City's Trust Requires Bullets and Handshakes, *New York Times*, April 5, 2003, p. B3; Keith B. Richburg, People in Basra Contest Official View of Siege, *Washington Post*, April 15, 2003, p. A13; Ryan Dilley, BBC News, Basra Bombing "Destroyed My Family," April 16, 2003; BBC News, Basra Utilities "Were Not Bombed," April 17, 2003.

and disarmament. House-to-house combat always will be exceptionally dangerous and destructive, but perhaps some of the worst features can be mitigated by tasers, rubber bullets, and systems that nondestructively penetrate walls to temporarily incapacitate those inside. Perhaps loud noises and blinding lights could have dissuaded the merely curious and driven away the casual hangers-on, enabling the troops to identify more readily those determined individuals who posed the genuine threat. When relief aid does come forward, it is obviously unacceptable to employ deadly force against those who urgently press forward for food or water; perhaps chemical NLWs could have helped ensure an orderly and fair distribution process, with less danger of uncontrolled rioting.

Antimateriel NLWs can provide distinct advantages too. Vehicle checkpoints established on a city's egress routes are notoriously vulnerable; the British might have benefitted from vehicle-stopping nets or electromagnetic pulse systems that could channelize or disable an oncoming car or truck that, for either legitimate or hostile reasons, ignored the traffic control directions. Other types of barrier systems might have protected important facilities from looting – instead of piling up an earthen berm around an oil company building (as the Iraqis did), and instead of fatally shooting five bank robbers (as the British did), NLWs might have quickly and easily created an impenetrable seal on vulnerable buildings.

Instead of catastrophically blowing up valuable infrastructure, perhaps NLWs such as slippery foam and carbon fibers could have enabled the invading force to put bridges, roadways, and public utilities out of commission only temporarily, permitting a more rapid return to service when the *fedayeen* left – and facilitating the occupiers' efforts to "win the hearts and minds" of the citizenry. A "soft kill" of the telephone system, the television apparatus, and other services likewise could have benefited the invaders in the not-so-very-long run. Regarding the episodic columns of troops and vehicles that bolted out of the city during the siege: if they really were impelled by threats against their families, instead of by misbegotten military strategy, it might well have been more desirable to disable and contain them, via caltrops and ignition-arresting systems, rather than inflict wholesale destruction and death. NLWs might have played a role even in operations undertaken to destroy captured enemy weaponry – a large ammunition dump at the Basra stadium might have been more productively sealed and disabled by nonexplosive means.

One potential NLW device was conspicuous by its absence, or at least by its nonuse. President Bush had authorized the deployment of non-lethal chemical munitions into the theater of conflict, where some had advocated their potential utility against entrenched resistance. The British colleagues, however, rejected any such maneuver as inconsistent with the Chemical Weapons Convention, and in any event, no chemicals – riot control devices or other – were ever applied by any side on the Iraqi battlefield.

In legal terms, the issue here centers on the law of armed conflict principles discussed in Chapter 3, especially the fundamental principles of avoidance of unnecessary suffering and the mandate for careful discrimination or distinction between combatants and civilians. The *fedayeen* and the Iraqi army manifestly did their best to violate those canons: they intermingled legitimate military targets with protected locations and people, and attempted to deter or frustrate the British – or to lure them into the sort of action that would further imperil the noncombatants. The British, on the other hand, did their best to comply with the customary international law – acknowledging that warfare, especially in an urban environment, can never be surgical, but accepting the responsibility to minimize the collateral damage.

In sum, the British patience in confronting Basra paid off. By waiting until the time was ripe, the U.K. forces avoided what might have been much more protracted and destructive urban combat, with devastating consequences for the invaders, the defenders, and the surrounding civilians. When the assault finally came, there was much less destruction of the city and much less antagonism between occupiers and residents than would have arisen otherwise.

Still, we cannot help but wonder whether judicious application of NLWs might have generated an even better outcome. The two-week delay in occupying the city was hardly cost-free: during that interval, the citizens suffered under the multiple burdens of a devastated municipal water system, rampant looting, and rapacious *fedayeen* forces that killed countless individuals. Anything that might have cracked the local resistance more quickly – that might have ended Basra's anarchy sooner and might have sped coalition forces on their campaign toward Baghdad and the toppling of Saddam – is worth exploring. And the combined firepower of aircraft, artillery, tanks, and other warfighters did, of course, damage the city and kill and injure innocent civilians – even if the toll was not as high as it might have been, each unintended casualty is regrettable.

Outside observers, and even the British forces themselves, frequently analogized between the ongoing difficulties in Basra and the much more protracted troubles in Northern Ireland. Many of the U.K. troops were veterans of that domestic conflict; they were experienced in the nuances of crowd control, the dangers of urban fighting, and the conundrum of providing civil services while promoting law and order – and they were intimately familiar with the role that judicious use of NLWs can play.

The final act of the saga of Basra, like that of Iraq itself, is still to be written. The plague of terrorism, the unquenched ambitions of Ba'athist loyalists, and the irregularities of local law and order remain outstanding hurdles. But even there, NLWs might play a role in enforcing legitimate authority without further inflaming tensions between occupier and occupied – as one British soldier put it, "We'd hate to win the war but lose the peace."[16]

[16] BBC News, British Plan Joint Patrols in Basra, April 12, 2003.

NINE

Cautionary Considerations

The implicit message of the previous chapters must not be over-read. The roster of emerging non-lethal weapon technologies might, at first, generate a breathless anticipation about future "bloodless conflict," in which American troops and police one day could prevail with only minimal costs to themselves, to innocent civilians, and even to the hostile forces. The five case studies, and the speculations about how NLWs of various sorts might have ameliorated the confrontations in Waco, Rwanda, Lima, Moscow, and Basra, might generate a knee-jerk mandate to develop, procure, and deploy more of those devices as soon as possible.

But there are important reasons to hesitate before blindly pursuing non-lethals. Three classes of caveats must be surveyed in any balanced consideration of the future of NLWs for police and military applications: concerns that might be labeled "operational" considerations about how the mechanisms might suit the realities of modern law enforcement and conflict; apprehensions about proliferation of the technologies to other, malign users; and the dangers of encouraging facile overreliance on force that must, even with non-lethal capabilities, be exercised with restraint.

A. OPERATIONAL CONSTRAINTS ON NON-LETHAL WEAPONS

The transition from drawing board to operational field is laden with impediments, and any of the NLW concepts we have discussed must address several potential pitfalls. This section briefly notes some of the constraints that NLWs (as any new weapon) must overcome – and, not coincidentally, some of the reasons why non-lethals have not yet succeeded in flooding the market for police and military arsenals.

Cost, for example, is a major consideration – any new system would have to justify its place in the funding queue, and the budgets for police and the armed services traditionally favor the tried-and-true technologies that might be displaced by unproven newcomers. New technologies seem inexorably to cost more than their predecessors, and any anticipated financial savings (e.g., from having to procure fewer units of the new, higher-quality items) often prove illusory.

Related are logistics concerns: if police and military would be required to maintain two sets of overlapping capabilities – NLWs alongside traditional lethal force – the burdens of transportation, maintenance, and supply increase. A police squad car, for example, can pack only so much equipment – and when the cop leaves the vehicle to investigate a threatening situation, how much can he or she conveniently carry? A military unit, likewise, would be doubly encumbered if it had to transport – and if each member had to haul into conflict – both lethal and non-lethal firearms; even the burden of lugging around two sets of ammunition may be considerable.

One possible solution (or at least a hoped-for quality in some NLW contexts) would be a "rheostatic" weapon, with which the user could select any particular level of force to apply in a specific confrontation. A rifle capable of adjusting its muzzle velocity, for example, could permit the shooter to adjust the speed of the projectile, depending upon the range to the target, thus reducing the likelihood that the rubber or beanbag bullet would deliver too strong a blow. Similarly, a weapon with two barrels could be devised to allow the user to toggle quickly between firing a conventional lethal bullet or a non-lethal electric shock dart.

Such combined effects weapons could maximize the user's flexibility without so much encumberence as having to bear dual firearms. On the other hand, they would exacerbate a danger that the soldier or police officer, in the heat of a tense, fast-breaking crisis, might inadvertently set the dials incorrectly or pull the wrong trigger, unleashing lethal power when non-lethal was intended, or vice versa. Already, a similar problem has occasionally emerged, with police mistaking their taser for their pistol, and accidentally firing the wrong type of force.

Another danger is the very real possibility that the NLWs will not perform as advertised – and the devices may err in either of two directions. First, a weapon might not prove to be reliably non-lethal; it might inflict fatal wounds or prove poisonous for too many people targeted by it. Second, at the opposite extreme, it might be ineffective, failing to disable or dissuade the target, compromising the mission and exposing the user to possibly lethal return fire.

Training is another formidable obstacle and cost. Obviously, police officers on the beat and soldiers in the field must always be properly instructed about any new weapons and afforded adequate opportunities to practice modified tactics before putting them to the test in operation. But that responsibility is even greater here than in other contexts: NLWs imply very different strategies for the application of force; these are not merely new tools, but the beginning of a new way of thinking about many law enforcement and military functions. The operators, therefore, will require careful guidance in the new doctrines and concepts of operations. Any weapon is subject to misuse, through misunderstanding or malice; thorough, repeated training and leadership can be the best bulwarks against misapplication of NLWs.

In addition, as with any other contemplated armament, any NLW system must pass the traditional tests of being sufficiently small, light, durable, mobile, and rugged for use in the field. It must not require elaborate support, maintenance, or fuel. It must act quickly, and preferably at a range sufficient to keep the user away from a rock-throwing crowd. It must be accurate, to specify a particular target, and capable of repeat firing at a reasonable rate. It must be immune to adverse weather conditions. It must not expose the user to undue smoke, noise, or other toxic or obnoxious effects. It must not unduly outrage public opinion. It must not create excessive pollution or other long-term safety hazards. Some NLW candidates can – or will soon be able to – pass these tests, but others will likely remain simply "pie in the sky."

We also have to think about NLWs in dynamic terms, anticipating the likely responses of other actors to our deployments of these new weapons. That is, are there simple, inexpensive countermeasures that would be available to a calculating opponent, enabling the targets to evade or blunt the NLW effects? The Davidians in Waco and the MRTA in Lima were equipped with rudimentary gas masks that afforded them some breathing space amid the CS; the occupiers of the Dubrovka Theater incident were not similarly foresightful, but after that experience, will Chechen terrorists routinely come to future missions with better protective devices? (There have been indications that the terrorists responsible for the school massacre at Beslan, Russia, in September 2004 did carry some gas masks.) In general, any NLW that is susceptible to efficient countermeasures will be of greatly reduced value – and we should anticipate the possibility of an action–reaction "arms race" model evolving with competitive innovations alternating between offensive and defensive capabilities.

Next, there is the "wimp factor" to consider: if our police and military forces come to utilize non-lethal force, and if that posture becomes known to their opponents, will that practice embolden the criminals and enemy troops to resist with even greater zeal? These targeted individuals might then rationally calculate that, if they defy official authority, the worst that could happen would be infliction of a painful or disabling blow, followed by detention – but reducing or eliminating the prospect of being shot to death might mitigate the instinct to surrender. It is not just a macho preference for traditional deadly force that sometimes inspires military and police to resist the notion of NLWs – in a world where violence is frequent and sometimes lethal, being armed with more firepower than your opponents is the traditional formula for success and sheer survival.[1]

Legal considerations, too, might impede the evolution toward NLWs. The treaties and statutes surveyed in Chapter 3 circumscribe certain weapons pathways, notably regarding lasers, chemicals, and biological agents. These are especially sensitive fields, and despite the hypothetical possibility that judicious application of non-lethal chemicals, for example, might humanely save some lives in particular wartime applications, skeptics wisely caution against the danger of undermining the essential arms control constraints of the Chemical Weapons Convention and the Biological Weapons

---

[1] Military personnel often assert a strong instinctual preference for the traditional power of overwhelming lethal force, expressing impatience and disinterest in anything perceived as "softer" than conventional bullets and bombs. See, e.g., W. Hays Parks, Non-Lethal Weapons: Musings from Experience, presentation to Council on Foreign Relations NLW Task Force, September 8, 2003, pp. 4–5 (quoting a Marine officer as saying that the only "non-lethal" weapon he needed was a Marine with his finger *outside* the trigger guard of his weapon).

Convention. Most military uses of chemical and biological agents, even for relatively benign NLW applications, are therefore simply off limits.

A different type of legal concern grows out of the constraints upon official violence reflected in both customary international law and domestic U.S. case law. That is, if police and the military are required, pursuant to various formulations, to utilize only "reasonable" or "proportionate" levels of force, would their future possession of NLW capabilities subtly shift that calculation? That is, if authorities possess non-lethal capabilities, might they become legally compelled to utilize those restrained approaches first, before resorting to traditional lethal means?[2]

Government officials, sensitive to this possibility, have already asserted their opposition to any such trend. The U.S. Department of Defense and NATO both have issued guidance asserting without reservation that self-defense remains the first touchstone for the military – if deadly force is authorized, there is absolutely no requirement or even recommendation that it be approached stepwise, starting with NLWs first. Non-lethal capability is intended to augment, not to displace, traditional weapons and does not alter

---

[2] A similar progression may be occurring with regard to precision-guided munitions. That is, as the United States develops sophisticated "smart bombs," capable of targeting particular locations with exquisite accuracy, and as these munitions become much more common in the arsenal, some argue that it may become inappropriate, illegitimate, and eventually illegal under humanitarian standards to use old-fashioned "dumb bombs," which create much more indiscriminate collateral damage through their imprecision. This purported requirement for using the best technology would not be imposed upon other countries that, because of inferior technology or defense budgets, did not procure the smart weaponry. John B. Alexander, *Future War: Non-Lethal Weapons in 21st Century Warfare* (1999) p. 197; Danielle L. Infeld, Precision-Guided Munitions Demonstrated Their Pinpoint Accuracy in Desert Storm: But Is a Country Obligated to Use Precision Technology to Minimize Collateral Civilian Injury and Damage? 26 *George Washington Journal of International Law and Economics* 109 (1992); Christopher B. Puckett, In This Era of "Smart Weapons," Is a State under an International Legal Obligation to Use Precision-Guided Technology in an Armed Conflict? 18 *Emory International Law Review* 645 (fall 2004).

existing standards for the employment of fully lethal force.[3] Likewise, domestic U.S. courts and other authorities reviewing police operations are traditionally deferential to use-of-force decisions, especially those made in exigent circumstances. The Supreme Court's focus on "reasonable," not necessarily "minimal," force makes a fine distinction – no cases suggest that police are obligated to procure nonlethal mechanisms for first use in a threatening and fluid situation.

Still, it is predictable that, as law enforcement and military agents acquire the ability to behave with a more deft touch – to immobilize, incapacitate, or deter, instead of to kill and destroy, and to do so with equal effectiveness and safety – the law may well creep in the direction of requiring them to proceed with the less deadly means first. And that preference may apply even in situations where the opposing forces – because of opposite decisions they made about what weaponry to procure – are not similarly constrained.

B. THE DANGER OF PROLIFERATION

It is not plausible to assume that American police and defense forces would proceed unilaterally into an NLW world. If the technology works; if it is cost-effective, sufficiently portable, and field-rugged; if it succeeds in overcoming resistance from opponents; and if it facilitates our forces' accomplishment of their assigned missions,

---

[3] Department of Defense Directive 3000.3, Policy for Non-Lethal Weapons, July 9, 1996, sec. 4.4–4.5; Joint Non-Lethal Weapons Directorate, U.S. Marine Corps, Joint Concept for Non-Lethal Weapons, January 5, 1998, p. 6; NATO Policy on Non-Lethal Weapons, Press Statement, October 13, 1999 ("Neither the existence, the presence nor the potential effect of Non-Lethal Weapons shall constitute an obligation to use Non-Lethal Weapons, or impose a higher standard for, or additional restrictions on, the use of lethal force"); Margaret-Anne Coppernoll, The Nonlethal Weapons Debate, 52 *Naval War College Review* 112, spring 1998, pp. 9–10.

then others will mimic our pattern. The imitators may not immediately develop devices that are quite as robust, sophisticated, or safe as what we field – but they may not need to set such high performance standards, and this "reverse engineering" may expose us to a variety of unwelcome new threats. As the Council on Foreign Relations' Task Force on Non-Lethal Weapons expressed it in 2003, as "the most open, technology-dependent, and vulnerable society" the United States may be particularly susceptible to NLW retaliation.[4]

One obvious proliferation danger arises from enemy militaries. Just as we might find advantages in inflicting illness, pain, and disorientation upon our opponents, so might they – and the result may leave our troops more vulnerable. A new international arms race in NLWs could further burden our military budget and complicate the battlefield – and there is no certainty that American inventiveness would perpetually ensure an edge for us. An entirely non-lethal war is surely not in sight; whether a conflict characterized by an asymmetric mixture of lethal and non-lethal capabilities would play out to American advantage is impossible to foresee. Already, several other countries are proceeding apace with their own NLW investigations; self-restraint on the part of the United States might not elicit a reciprocal response from them at this point, but it is certainly clear that if we pioneer the field, others – including potential adversaries – will not willingly cede the entire realm of NLWs to us.[5]

---

[4] Council on Foreign Relations, Independent Task Force (Malcolm Wiener, chair), Non-Lethal Technologies: Military Options and Implications (1995), p. 74.

[5] James C. Duncan, A Primer on the Employment of Non-Lethal Weapons, 45 *Naval Law Review* (1998), pp. 1, 11–12 ("Around the world, many nations are creating non-lethal weapon systems. . . . There will always be foreign governments and terrorists groups who will mimic the non-lethal technology as it is developed [in the United States]"); Steve Metz, Non-Lethality and the Revolution in Military Affairs, in Malcolm Dando (ed.), Non-Lethal Weapons: Technological and Operational Prospects, Jane's online special report (November 2000), ch. 2 ("Nearly every advanced state has at least begun to explore the integration of non-lethality in their armed forces, and many have elaborate programmes to develop non-lethal weapons and the operational concepts to use them"); Nick Lewer and Tobias Feakin, Perspectives and Implications for the Proliferation of

Terrorists, too, might someday piggyback upon the government's NLW research and development work. If (as seems inevitable) the NLW technology slips, sooner or later, into the commercial marketplace (or the black marketplace), how might terrorists conspire to adapt the ADS system, the vortex ring generator, or the microwave engine-stalling apparatus for their pernicious objectives? Reportedly, some of the 9/11 hijackers used Mace or other disabling chemical sprays to assist in commandeering the fateful aircraft. Other systems, such as plastic stun guns or advanced non-lethal chemical-emitting devices, might be particularly pernicious in evading airport metal detectors or devices (or dogs) that can sniff out conventional firearms. As Robin Coupland has observed regarding NLW chemicals, "The same agents may be as useful, if not more so, for taking hostages than releasing hostages, or for spreading terror than deterring it."[6]

Another, equally problematic, form of proliferation would be to domestic criminals. Surely, if people are going to rob banks and convenience stores, it would be better for everyone involved if they did so with tasers and pepper spray, rather than with automatic weapons – but would the easy availability of non-lethal force lead to an even greater incidence of that antisocial behavior? If criminals acquired the ability to immobilize taxi drivers or people on the street – and, a fortiori, if they could instantly but temporarily paralyze everyone in a bank or other building with a future variant of an acoustic wave system – would they yield to that temptation

Non-Lethal Weapons in the Context of Contemporary Conflict, Security Interests and Arms Control, in Nick Lewer (ed.), *The Future of Non-Lethal Weapons: Technologies, Operations, Ethics, and Law* (2002), pp. 127–40 (noting that 110 countries deploy non-lethal riot control agents, and presenting a case study of India's use of tear gas and other crowd-control mechanisms).

6 Robin M. Coupland, Incapacitating Chemical Weapons: A Year after the Moscow Theatre Siege, 362 *Lancet*, October 25, 2003, p. 1346.

even more frequently, leading to an enlarged and further empowered criminal force?[7]

Finally, another category of proliferation causes great concern: the possible spread of pain-inducing NLW technology to human rights abusers. As the U.S. Department of State annually reports, a great many countries around the world still rely upon horrific practices of torture and punishment – either to coerce confessions and information from criminal suspects or to violate, agonize, and deter political opponents or disfavored religious or social groups. Many of these torturers satisfy themselves with the most primitive forms of barbarism, through whips, clubs, food deprivation, and the like, but some have come to rely upon more sophisticated – and often Western-supplied – implements such as electric shock devices. What additional horrors could they inflict if their arsenals were supplemented with tools such as pepper spray that could be so easily misused? The millimeter wave devices, for example, could inflict outrageous pain, especially upon someone who was physically restrained, unable to retreat and avoid the beam – and they could do so without inflicting any visible wounds or other permanent harm that subsequent investigators could detect and document. In the same vein, it is chilling to note that four of the Americans implicated in the notorious abuse of Iraqi prisoners in 2004 were disciplined specifically for the excessive use of force involving the unauthorized application of tasers against defenseless detainees.[8]

---

[7] Already, NLWs have occasionally been adapted for criminal purposes – to disarm a victim, to effectuate an escape, etc. Shoplifting Suspect Squirts Pepper Spray at Officer, Motorist, IndyChannel, August 3, 2004; Police Blotter, *Palm Beach Post,* August 4, 2004 (OC allegedly used in attempted robbery of convenience store); North Side Woman Stabs Acquaintance, *Pittsburgh Post-Gazette,* August 4, 2004 (in a fight, one woman used pepper spray to disarm her opponent, then seized the opponent's knife and stabbed her with it).

[8] Amnesty International, Arming the Torturers: Electric Shock Torture and the Spread of Stun Technology, March 1997; Amnesty International, USA – Market Leader in the Torture Trade, June 2001 (detailing U.S. production and export of electroshock

C. THE POSSIBILITY OF OVERRELIANCE ON NON-LETHAL WEAPONS

Finally, there is a danger that NLWs might work too well – or at least be perceived by the political leadership as succeeding so fully that the existing (and already quite fragile) constraints upon the use of force were dissipated. That is, if national authorities (wrongly) relied upon the illusion that future NLWs could permit the United States to project its power into international crises with appreciably less cost in terms of lives and property, would they be tempted to exercise that power more often? Would American troops find themselves deployed with even greater frequency into tumultuous, perhaps unwinnable, conflicts, because of the facile confidence that non-lethal force would offer a cheap, bloodless triumph?

On the law enforcement side, would an enhanced arsenal of NLWs prompt officials to send police or FBI into harm's way too quickly, fueling an impatience that should yield, instead, to a more judicious self-restraint and prolonged negotiations? Would an illusion about a completely non-lethal capability lull us into a false sense that police should immediately exercise their ability to "do something" in a crisis, instead of waiting for calmer options?

A related concern: the adoption of additional non-lethal capabilities, consciously translated from military into law enforcement applications, might intensify an ongoing process of "militarization" of the police. SWAT teams already have led that progression, both in the United States and elsewhere, and the effectiveness of those enhanced weapons and tactics is invaluable in certain situations.

weapons and restraints); Steve Wright, The Role of Sub-Lethal Weapons in Human Rights Abuse, in Nick Lewer (ed.), *The Future of Non-Lethal Weapons: Technologies, Operations, Ethics, and Law* (2002), pp. 75–86; U.S. Department of Defense, News Transcript, Presenter: Lawrence Di Rita, December 8, 2004.

But surely something is also lost when a community departs increasingly from an older, simpler model of less-forceful policing. There is evidence that violence – even the appearance of readiness for violence – by law enforcement can serve counterproductively to elicit a violent response from a crowd that might otherwise tone itself down.[9] If police come to possess what they see as a fine-grained ability to modulate their use of force, and if they accordingly sometimes turn to available non-lethal force when they might otherwise have had no real power to do anything at all, might the display of NLWs perversely serve to inflame the mob's passions and escalate the controversy?

Finally, a similar issue arises at the tactical level of individual police and military operations in the field. That is, the ready access to an array of effective NLWs may allow the uniformed personnel on the street more leeway to "shoot first and ask questions later." There are already disturbing suggestions that police, newly armed with tasers, utilize that level of force with surprising frequency – observers applaud the reduced reliance upon lethal firearms, but worry that law enforcement officials are becoming too "quick on the trigger" with electricity, in a situation where even lower levels of force, and greater levels of patience, might suffice.[10]

---

[9] Report of the National Advisory Commission on Civil Disorders, 1968, p. 330 (noting that "use of excessive force – even an inappropriate display of weapons – may be inflammatory and lead to even worse disorder," and quoting a FBI riot control manual as cautioning that unwarranted use of official force can incite a mob to further violence and prolong a disturbance).

[10] Gwen Shaffer, Force Multiplier, New Republic, August 2, 2004, pp. 19, 20 (quoting sociology professor John Noakes, "There's a perception that less lethal weapons are a good thing because no one wants to see cops using billy clubs. But this new technology is frightening because now the police don't have to exercise restraint"); Alex Berenson, As Police Use of Tasers Soars, Questions over Safety Emerge, New York Times, July 18, 2004, p. A1 (a study in Orange County, Florida, reported that police officers used pepper spray and batons much less frequently after they were also equipped with tasers, but their increased reliance upon the electrical stun guns more than compensated for the decreases in other implements, and total incidents of the use of police force increased by 58 percent).

In a dangerous, uncertain, and fast-moving milieu, soldiers and law enforcement personnel might welcome tools that reduce the adverse consequences of erroneous, off-target, or premature firing: NLWs could minimize the dangers of fratricide and of striking innocent civilians. Instead of having to sit back passively and absorb the first blow, police and military could take the risk of seizing the initiative with NLWs. But the question remains: Do we really want our protectors to become more proactive in this fashion? Is there an offsetting danger that NLWs would inspire too much quickness on the trigger, spurring anticipatory action when greater restraint would still be the wiser course?

TEN

Recommendations and Conclusions

It is difficult to generalize about non-lethal weapons; there is so much diversity in the objectives, current status, and future prospects of the various systems. Proponents sometimes refer casually to the "family" of NLW programs, but that vocabulary overstates their commonality – the different breeds of NLWs are not really closely related, and each must be evaluated on a careful, case-by-case basis for its individual feasibility, legality, and wisdom. Some NLW devices are familiar, having been successfully operated for years; others are just now on the cusp of deployment; still others appear only dimly on the horizon – and a few have already been discarded.

By the same token, perhaps it would be intellectually cleaner not to speak of a category of "non-lethal weapons" at all – if the entrants in this category have so little in common, and if each must be assessed separately, perhaps they should simply be labeled "weapons," and not generically distinguished from any others under that overarching heading. That notion has some appeal; in the abstract, NLWs are no more and no less than "weapons," and the same rules ought to apply to them as to all others.

But there is much to be gained by exploring the field, or subfield, of non-lethal arms, apart from all the other types of weapons, and by conceptualizing NLWs as a distinct genre. That is, there is something new and different going on here – the conscious effort to create capabilities that have not existed previously (or not to nearly the current and anticipated extent). These enterprises do have something in common, and we would be overlooking an important development if we merely chalked up all the NLW programs as indistinguishable from other types of weapons. Military and police forces are on the threshold of acquiring important new capacities; these revolutionary technologies may augur correspondingly altered roles and functions, and concerted attention to the field of NLWs can help illuminate the choices we now face.

To that end, I offer ten recommendations for future U.S. policy.

I. INTENSIFY THE OVERALL NON-LETHAL WEAPON EFFORT

First, and at the most basic level, I recommend that the United States pursue NLWs with increased vigor. There is genuine promise for a host of valuable applications at home and abroad, offering overdue assistance in addressing some of the most vexing police and military use-of-force dilemmas. Of course, not all NLWs are equally propitious – inevitably, some will be winnowed out, and others will survive the competitive battles for resources, acceptance, and public approval. But the first approach at this point is simply to do more – to invest more time, attention, and dollars into the nascent NLW revolution.

This upgraded effort demands two complementary strategies for pursuing not only (a) the "low-hanging fruit" of those NLW capabilities that are already close to operational, perhaps needing just one more bureaucratic and funding push before they can be finalized and provided to awaiting troops and police in the field, but also (b) the longer-lead-time, high-payoff possibilities that will require more sustained research and development, but that carry the potential for paradigm-shifting impact. The JNLWD's development and distribution of the NLW "capability sets" is a good illustration of the former approach, providing a quick, basically off-the-shelf set of equipment that at least can introduce the concept of non-lethal force and address immediate needs. Conversely, the persistent funding of the VMADS millimeter wave system is an example of the latter concept, steadfastly supporting a transformational technology for a decade or more in the hope that the ultimate payoff will prove worthwhile.

Notably, some rudimentary NLWs are already in use by U.S. forces in Afghanistan and Iraq, performing both antipersonnel and antimateriel functions. Tasers and pellet guns have been used in prison camps and to protect convoys, while netting barriers have proven useful in stopping vehicles for checkpoint inspection. These examples represent merely the tip of an iceberg; with a little imagination and a bit more procurement, NLWs of various sorts could help accomplish a variety of delicate and challenging missions in and around the scene of combat.

2. UPGRADE THE U.S. GOVERNMENT NON-LETHAL WEAPON ENTERPRISE

In light of that potential (and, even more, the established record of initial successes), it is particularly striking that the NLW commitments to date from both the Department of Defense and the Department of Justice have been so paltry. The Joint Non-Lethal Weapons Directorate, in particular, must be reinvigorated and expanded; with its current budget and staffing, it can not truly serve the "Johnny Appleseed" role of propagating NLW concepts and programs throughout the Pentagon. JNLWD must now be upgraded and empowered to provide more leadership to the military services in identifying and pursuing promising NLW leads, and to permit augmented interaction with domestic law enforcement agencies and with foreign allies. Any specific dollar figure would be largely arbitrary at this point, but we should think in terms of an order-of-magnitude increase over the current JNLWD allotment of roughly $45 million per year. Likewise, the Department of Justice ought to strengthen the National Institute of Justice, allowing it the funding and the prominence necessary to make a genuine contribution to NLW development. The need for a central facilitating authority is even greater on the law enforcement side than on the military side; the eighteen thousand state and local police, sheriffs, corrections agencies, etc., are simply too scattered and too diverse (and many of them are too small) to support indigenous research and development programs. If the wealth of experience of these multiple authorities is to be effectively marshaled and enlarged, the NIJ will have to step up.

A third federal bureaucratic player is also cautiously slipping one toe into NLWs, and ought to be encouraged to proceed more emphatically. The Department of Homeland Security (DHS), tasked with a bewildering array of domestic responsibilities for preventing and responding to domestic emergencies, is beginning to recognize the potential value of NLWs for a range of complex missions such as crowd control and protection of sensitive installations, where both strength and delicacy are required. DHS made news recently when it rejected the procurement of tasers, because of concerns about the safety of the electrical systems,[1] but it may well come to adopt other NLWs, in partnership with DoD and DoJ, as they mature. Challenges such as enforcing a quarantine, in the event of a domestic chemical or biological weapons emergency or a natural catastrophe such as an avian influenza pandemic, could demand NLWs to

---

[1] Kevin Johnson, Federal Bureaus Reject Stun Guns, *USA Today*, March 18, 2005, p. A3.

prevent agitated civilians from entering or exiting a defined "hot zone," and the department's existing tools seem inadequate to the challenge.

A key aspect of an expanded federal NLW enterprise should be to ensure a greater degree of cooperation and coordination among the various NLW stakeholder agencies. That collaboration was supposed to have been effectuated years ago, beginning with the post-Waco exchanges between Attorney General Janet Reno and Secretaries of Defense Les Aspin and William Perry. But the integration of the efforts of JNLWD and NIJ has never been as profound as it could have been, and the military and law enforcement sides of the U.S. government NLW enterprises still seem oddly isolated.

Now is the time to rectify that lapse, and to intensify the interaction among all participants. Each agency brings something special to the table: the Pentagon (and to some extent, DHS) can offer deeper pockets, established access to high-technology research and development laboratories, and expertise with funding and administering large, long-term procurement programs; the Department of Justice, via the police departments across the country, can supply the wealth of prior experience and the laboratory for further experimentation with promising NLW concepts.

No doubt, the two sides of the NLW enterprise will continue to have different emphases and areas of specialization – the obvious contrasts between all-out international combat and domestic policing inevitably generate important differences in equipment and tactics. But there should be more cross-fertilization. When General Zinni led his Marines into Somalia in 1995, he had to rely largely upon commercial, off-the-shelf equipment and upon the Los Angeles County Sheriff's Department experts for NLW training and tactics. That is an odd pattern and should not have been forced into implementation on an emergency basis.

This is not a plea to blur the important lines between police and military – each will continue to have its unique needs and strengths, its distinct priorities and missions. To note one obvious difference, a prime desiderata for military NLWs would be longer-range systems, to enable soldiers to engage hostile targets at standoff distances; in police work, however, most encounters with the citizenry in fact occur at very short range, but with an even lower tolerance for lethality.

In the same vein, increased NLW interaction between DoD and DoJ should not be interpreted as a call to further "militarize" law enforcement. Surprisingly, however, in may instances, it is local SWAT teams that have become the greatest proponents of augmented NLW options. They, even more than other police units, have had the first-hand occasion to appreciate the flexibility and breadth of novel NLWs as an intermediate capacity between verbal instructions and lethal violence.

So there appears to be a natural, but still largely unexploited, synergy between the two types of NLW applications, and both sides – military as well as police – would benefit from greater interaction.

3. DEMAND MORE EFFECTIVE LEADERSHIP
ON NON-LETHAL WEAPONS

There is a conundrum about NLWs: in spite of all the potential, in spite of all the research and development, in spite of the demonstrated record of success, why have NLWs not yet achieved a greater level of public and governmental support, adoption, and visibility?

At a very basic level, NLWs have not yet broken through the consciousness of the key players. Military and civilian leaders at DoD have routinely proven themselves disinterested; Congress has not seized the issue; the general public is only vaguely and episodically aware of pending breakthroughs. Somehow, that situation must be changed; the relevant players need to understand more fully what is at stake here and what can be accomplished.

Some of this insight could be achieved through "top down" direction – senior officials could order additional resources to be devoted to this promising, revolutionary field, laying the groundwork for benefits that would be realized years hence. Alternatively, some of the impetus could be felt from the "bottom up," as the military services and police forces seek better arms for their gun-toters in the field.

Looked at another way, NLWs should be a subject of both "technology push" (with research and development laboratories inventing attractive new systems to offer to the military and police forces) and "demand pull" (with individual soldiers and police officers asking their superiors for improved tools to achieve their assigned objectives). The problem to date is that the inventors do not seem to understand exactly what augmented capabilities the fielded forces would most appreciate, and the individual cops and soldiers are not aware of what technology might be able to offer. Leadership, therefore, is necessary to ensure a better matchup, so the laboratories can respond to, and even anticipate, the demands from the field, and the front lines can articulate better what innovations would best equip them to deal with the novel pressures they now face.

There is therefore something of a chicken-and-egg problem here. As described by Marine Corps Lieutenant General Jan Huly, captains of private industry have been too slow to invest in developing new NLWs, because they have not yet seen substantial commitments of money in government procurement. On the other hand, the military, which now has authorization to spend more public funds on

NLW purchases, has been frustrated by finding relatively little yet offered by commercial industry. That "cycle of failure" must be interrupted; again it is leadership that must be applied to close the gap between financial risk and proven capabilities.[2]

One specific measure that could be of immediate value would be to increase the role of NLWs in "war games" undertaken by the military and in comparable simulation exercises created by DHS, DoJ, and local police. These sorts of training events – some styled as "tabletop" or seminar room hypotheticals, to train leaders in crisis decision making; some involving soldiers, first responders, and others in field drills – are essential in developing new institutional and individual capabilities, and they are routinely undertaken. But NLWs are not regularly included in the array of tools and tactics to be studied; there are just not enough NLW experts to go around. JNLWD, for example, conspicuously lacks the manpower to send representatives to a sufficient number of such programs.

These exercises offer an unparalleled opportunity to spread the word about NLWs within the most relevant communities. A dedicated commitment will be required to expand the presence of NLWs in systematic training, to help both top leaders and working-level operators to understand what the emerging capabilities could do for them.

It is ironic that the world of NLWs is today characterized simultaneously by (a) ignorance, indifference, or even skepticism on the part of those who do not yet know much about NLWs, and (b) impatience and frustration by the handful of NLW experts, who object that progress has been too slow in realizing the transformational

[2] Neil Davidson and Nick Lewer, Bradford Non-Lethal Weapons Research Project, Research Report No. 7, May 2005, p. 14; Joe Pappalardo, Homeland Defense Plan Favors Non-Lethal Technology and Researchers Fill Data Gaps for Less-than-Lethal Weapons, 89 *National Defense*, June 2005, p. 49.

potential of the new devices. The Council on Foreign Relations, which through its task forces has monitored NLW activities as closely as anyone over the past decade, has both heralded the arrival of the new systems and complained that the promised arrival of "tomorrow's weapons" seems continuously postponed. Now is the time to start delivering on those promises.

4. DEVELOP A VIGOROUS PUBLIC OUTREACH STRATEGY

Public visibility is an important ingredient for public acceptance, and that outreach component has been conspicuously lacking for NLWs. The government should therefore now undertake a much greater public relations and education program in support of the new technologies. In the same vein, congressional relations efforts must be intensified – too few members and senior staffers on Capitol Hill have more than passing familiarity with the concept of NLWs, and that invisibility has stultified potential alliances.

For whatever reason, the traditional strategy at DoD has not been to publicize the efforts and achievements in NLWs. Perhaps fearing that any program for new weapons at this time might elicit knee-jerk opposition, the Pentagon deliberately has kept a low profile on non-lethal activities across the board. But the consequence has not been sub rosa success; instead, public watchdog groups have challenged the wisdom, legality, and success of various JNLWD enterprises, and the directorate has been constrained about putting forward its own perspectives.

NIJ has likewise sailed beneath the public radar; it, too, would benefit from greater visibility. Being more transparent with our NLW research and development programs can help "sell" the legitimacy of the undertaking, enhancing public awareness of the concept of NLWs and securing broad acceptance of the undertaking.

Three specific points should be noted for any such NLW public affairs campaign. First, it is important not to overpromise. Even the name "non-lethal" can be misleading; what we really mean here is "less often lethal" or "reduced probability of lethality." No one should be under the illusion that there can ever be an iron-clad guaranty of safety for any weapon, barrier, or other device. There is no magic chemical potion that will instantly disable hostage takers without jeopardizing their victims; there is no impact munition that will disarm or deter reliably without danger of unintended consequences. Our enthusiasm for what some of the emerging NLWs might be able to accomplish should not obscure the fact that unproven technologies often fail, or at least disappoint – and if we tout the near-mystical capabilities of a device that is still only on a drawing board, we will discredit the genuine accomplishments offered by realistic new devices.

Second, it is now time (or well past time) to engage the critics of NLWs. To date, the U.S. government and other NLW proponents mostly have tried to ignore or exclude those who doubt the value of NLWs, who challenge the legality of chemical weapons-related efforts, or who simply remain skeptical about the entire field. That resistance is now obsolete, and the JNLWD and NIJ ought to reach out to the activists in the Sunshine Project, Amnesty International, the Federation of American Scientists, the Bradford Non-Lethal Weapons Research Project, the Red Cross, the ACLU, and others. There is a great deal of expertise in those institutions – and, even more striking, some objectives and concerns that the government shares. We all want the weapons to work – to be safe, effective, and legal – and to contribute to wise public policy. Constructive dialogue with critics across the spectrum of political and scientific perspectives might yield a surprising degree of common ground.

Third, as an exception to the general bias in favor of public disclosure, it is worth noting that some selected NLW programs might need to remain "black," as part of a classified effort by the military or intelligence services. Sometimes – not often – it is important to conceal the unusual antipersonnel and antimateriel programs now underway, to provide cover for a successful counterterrorism or other effort. But the overwhelming majority of police and military capabilities need not be so shrouded from public scrutiny.

Overall, the public relations battle is one that NLWs should be able to win – this is, after all, a quest for a more humanitarian mechanism, a device for accomplishing U.S. objectives with less bloodshed and destruction. But to succeed in the public relations arena, JNLWD, DoJ, and other proponents will have to get into the game; to date, their silence has been deafening.

It is, of course, far from guaranteed that the community will immediately warm to these unfamiliar technologies – chemicals, biologicals, and blinding lasers have helped put the worst foot forward for NLWs, and it is hardly surprising that many people greet the prospect of new, still-mysterious weapons with distrust. But in the long run, rubber bullets are better for use against crowds than are real bullets; a soft kill of an enemy power plant will play better than would more permanent destruction; the VMADS millimeter wave system, if it is used properly, will not horrify people the way that bloodshed or other oppressive devices do.

5. COORDINATE NON-LETHAL WEAPON
PROGRAMS WITH ALLIES

The U.S. military has already engaged in some rudimentary NLW programs of cooperation with other countries. Collaborative war game exercises with the United Kingdom in 2000 were mutually beneficial, and NATO has demonstrated interest in non-lethal capabilities in general.[3] But much more should be done in this area, to share both the benefits of the technology and financial costs of creating it.

In an era when many military operations are undertaken only in coalition with other countries, shared access to advanced NLWs is vital. Our partners will need to understand and apply the same devices U.S. forces may use to control crowds, secure buildings, and enforce checkpoints, and the same training, rules of engagement, and "concept of operations" ought to govern our shared activities.

Whether engaged in all-out fighting, in "military operations other than war," or in civil administration and law enforcement, American and allied forces will find NLWs of various sorts useful – but they can be wielded in the most effective, concerted fashion only if we have taken the time in advance to share the equipment and to train with each other.

6. ADDRESS EMERGING DOMESTIC AND INTERNATIONAL LEGAL ISSUES

The new realm of NLWs and the changed circumstances of modern threats combine to raise or exacerbate a host of international and domestic legal issues that demand reappraisal.

For example, the scourge of superterrorism by nonstate actors and the greatly enhanced danger of proliferated catastrophic weapons

[3] US/UK Non-Lethal Weapons Wargaming Program, Policy Seminar Assessment, January 19–20, 2000; War Game Three Assessment, September 12–15, 2000; and Executive Seminar Assessment, November 30, 2000.

of mass destruction require us to reexamine the traditional protocols of the law of armed conflict for the modern era. The reality of frequent "military operations in urban terrain" now results in a battle space teeming with civilians – some innocent bystanders to the carnage, some unwilling hostages, some covert fighters. When enemy combatants do not routinely honor the requirements to differentiate and separate themselves from civilians, the demands upon our forces become much more complex.

NLWs sometimes may offer a partial solution to those puzzles, but the meshing of new technology with rules fashioned in a different era for a different brand of combat will not be easy or automatic. The core principles of the law of war surely will retain their vitality, but we are now pressed to think in different ways about how to apply them in unfamiliar contexts. Novel NLW capabilities such as VMADS or a future acoustic system may be able to "clear a space" by compelling everyone – civilians and fighters alike – to evacuate a neighborhood, avoiding the horrendous cost of street-by-street combat. Implicit in that tactic, however, is the direct and general targeting of a pain-inducing weapon system upon civilians located at the periphery of an engagement – not at all a comfortable procedure within the realm of traditional war fighting that demands discriminating, proportionate uses of force.

Likewise, uncertainty persists regarding the articulation of appropriate "rules of engagement" for specific NLWs. If rubber bullets, pepper spray, or tasers can contribute to a mission, but if they also carry some finite possibility for inflicting mortal wounds, where unfortunate variables apply, what standards should govern? Would we instruct soldiers to fire the disabling rounds only in circumstances in which use of fully deadly force would also be authorized – or does that sort of restriction defeat the whole purpose of NLWs? If we do "lower the standards" for an application of force when non-lethal means will apply, how much reduction is appropriate? And would we require that non-lethal means be applied *first*, prior to a resort to deadly power?

Fresh insights from the legal community are required in the domestic context as well. The new mission of protecting homeland security against a variety of foreign and domestic threats is a most challenging requirement, engaging both military and law enforcement assets and a variety of other first responders, and the dividing line between military operations and law enforcement becomes increasingly fuzzy. It is terribly complicated to have to prepare to battle terrorists both at home and abroad, to have to conduct dangerous missions in the midst of civilian populations, and to be trained and equipped to undertake both lethal and non-lethal missions interchangeably. But that complexity is now a fact of life – regrettably, but unavoidably, our military and police guardians must now adapt themselves and their weaponry to the confusing, still-evolving threats and missions, and NLWs can make a unique contribution.

Ordinary law enforcement standards, too, must be reexamined with the enhanced NLWs in mind, and the conundrums do not admit easy answers. For example, in most states the commission of a crime through use of a lethal firearm is punished more severely than would be a similar act aided only by a NLW such as a taser or pepper spray. That strategy has the sensible effect of positively reinforcing less-deadly activity and deterring the most dangerous and violent permutations. But if more powerful NLWs proliferate, and if criminals become proficient at adapting black market or knock-off versions of millimeter wave systems, non-lethal netting for individuals and vehicles, sticky foams, etc., should the criminal justice system respond with greater severity? Will NLWs otherwise come back to haunt us in the domestic sphere?

7. PRESERVE THE ACCOMPLISHMENTS OF ARMS CONTROL TREATIES

NLWs also may challenge some of the fundamental tenets of arms control, and vigilance is required to prevent those adverse implications too.

In particular, we should assiduously avoid imperiling the slender reeds of the Chemical Weapons Convention, the Biological Weapons Convention, the Convention on Certain Conventional Weapons, and other worthy but fragile standards of international law that might be jeopardized by unconstrained NLW developments. Riot control agents, for example, have long exerted a tantalizing allure for military applications, and it is undeniable that in particular scenarios, they might prove a transitory boon. But the world consciously decided, for manifest good reasons, not to go down that treacherous pathway, and even if the treaties were crafted long before modern NLWs arose, we should take pains not to unravel that global consensus. Biological devices too – conceivable for both antipersonnel and antimateriel NLW applications – might have superficial appeal in a number of scenarios, but should remain off the table. Chemical and biological weapons are among the few areas where international law has been laboriously emplaced to restrict combat violence – those taboos should not be relaxed, and we should not tolerate undo "leakage" from treaty-permitted use of chemicals in law enforcement or military operations other than war.

More generally, we should be loathe to trigger a new form of international arms race, with countries voraciously competing to invent and deploy still more types of novel military capability. Humanity already has sufficient means to conduct warfare; it hardly needs new tools, even non-lethal tools, to further those practices. For that reason, some have already called for treaty negotiations looking to regulate NLWs, or at least to channel the emerging programs into safer, less provocative directions.[4] At this point, however, that instinct seems premature; articulation of any international restrictions on NLW development should be held in abeyance until we have a better idea of what capabilities may be possible, and which may be unnecessarily dangerous.

On the other hand, it is not too early to generate certain non-proliferation restrictions on NLWs that are subject to tragic misuse. For example, tools and techniques that inflict pain to ensure compliance (e.g., the millimeter wave apparatus, tasers, and strong acoustic wave devices) should presumptively not be exported or otherwise provided to countries that are known to engage in torture of domestic minority groups, political dissidents, or the criminally accused. Those human rights abusing regimes should not ordinarily be eligible to receive even non-lethal technology that could be applied to perpetuate those injustices.

8. INSIST UPON RIGOROUS, REALISTIC TESTING FOR CANDIDATE NON-LETHAL WEAPONS

The absence or deficit in current testing algorithms is one of the major shortfalls in existing NLW programs, and much more rigorous, thorough, and realistic examination must be undertaken of the

---

[4] Rupert Pengelley, Wanted: A Watch on Non-Lethal Weapons, *Jane's International Defense Review*, April 1, 1994; Jürgen Altmann, Non-Lethal Weapons Technologies: The Case for Independent Scientific Analysis, in Nick Lewer (ed.), *The Future of Non-Lethal Weapons: Technologies, Operations, Ethics, and Law* (2002), pp. 112, 122–3 (calling for "preventive arms control" measures to limit the qualitative improvement in NLWs).

safety and effectiveness of candidate and future weapons systems for police and the military.

Some manufacturers have occasionally instituted internal testing programs of one sort or another for their marketed NLWs, but these have been largely episodic and anecdotal – exposing random volunteers or animals to the device or chemical in question and observing the results. These in-house experiments are obviously no substitute for truly independent, broad-scope testing and seem, frankly, to be mere adjuncts to the firms' sales efforts.

Governmental assessment programs to date have been little better. Local police departments have few resources to devote to systematic research and little internal facility at critical assessment of a company's proffered analyses. Likewise, the federal offices at NIJ and JNLWD (even with an alphabet soup of human effects panels, centers, and boards) are confined mostly to merely reviewing the safety and efficacy testing conducted elsewhere; the agencies have few funds and little internal capacity for sponsoring or undertaking the type of laboratory and field testing necessary to validate the proposed weapons on a realistic basis.[5]

What is necessary for most proposed NLW devices would be punctilious, long-term inspection of the full range of conditions under which the weapon would be used and the entire population that might be exposed to it – comparable, perhaps, to the testing required of food, drugs, electrical appliances, and other consumer products. At the moment, we do not even have a common vocabulary – different suppliers, for example, market all manner of blunt impact

---

[5] JNLWD and the individual U.S. military services have instituted elaborate procedures for vetting the health impact of new NLW concepts, including establishing a Human Effects Process Action Team, a Human Effects Review Board, a Human Effects Center of Excellence, and a Human Effects Advisory Panel.

munitions, some laced with OC packets of different strengths, with different nomenclature, confusing the public and confounding efforts at comparison shopping.[6] In some areas – electric stun guns may be the best example – the time has come for enforceable national standards on design and manufacturing. Taser weapons now largely escape effective federal regulation, because the darts are expelled from the device by compressed nitrogen gas, instead of by gunpowder, thereby dodging the legal definition of a covered "firearm." Many individual states regulate these arms in one manner or another, but this patchwork quilt of enactments precludes comprehensive treatment. Where self-regulation by the industry has proven patently insufficient, where the instrument carries both great promise and apparent dangers, and where the particular tool has attained such a high level of prominence within the national market, a more comprehensive licensing approach is mandated.[7]

Nothing is more important for the future health of the concept of NLWs than satisfactory human effects assessment. We have to do more to ensure that the devices do work as advertised, that the long-term and cumulative effects are well characterized, and that the weapons reliably earn the moniker of "non-lethal"; existing informal testing mechanisms too often fail to provide those assurances.

[6] See Christine Chinlund, The Perils of Imprecision, *Boston Globe*, December 20, 2004, p. A15 (describing standardless terminology colloquially applied to pepper spray guns, pellets, balls, and other projectiles).
[7] See Donald K. Stern, Report of the Commission Investigating the Death of Victoria Snelgrove, appointed by Boston Police Commissioner Kathleen M. O'Toole, May 25, 2005. (A Boston-area student was killed accidentally when police fired pepper pellets that hit her in the eye during celebrations following a 2004 Red Sox victory. The panel investigating the incident, observing the chaos surrounding NLWs, called for national standards for testing and use by police of crowd-control weapons.)

9. CONDUCT MORE RIGOROUS TRAINING FOR
NON-LETHAL WEAPON USERS

We must train, as well as equip, the police and military forces, so the new NLWs will be used in a manner consistent with the underlying intentions. In too many cases, the existing training procedures for local police officers leave much to be desired: some rely too heavily upon the manufacturer for instruction, some depend upon unaccountable third-party commercial services, some use poorly trained internal instructors, and some still depend upon self-training, with officers simply firing the NLWs at each other, to experience first-hand the power and pain of the system.

Some police and military units, of course, have instituted rigorous and comprehensive training programs, and these should serve as models for the others, but there is little standardization and usually no way to assess the adequacy of the program (other than post-mortem inspection, after something has gone drastically awry).

Training is essential regarding both *how* to use a new weapon and *when* to use it. That is, officers need not only to become proficient at the mechanics of arming and aiming, but also to understand what the particular NLW device can and cannot do for them. They must understand the applicable "rules of engagement," to appreciate the circumstances under which non-lethal force, as well as conventional lethal force, can be invoked. Associated with those demands would be instruction on maintaining and storing the equipment, testing it for continued effectiveness, cleaning up after its employment, and treating the victims after exposure. Soldiers and police need to understand fully the range of likely effects of the weapons, the contraindications against using them in certain situations, and the likely countermeasures that opponents might adopt. In many instances, those demands will be minimal and the training obvious, but in some NLW applications, the instruction can be quite demanding.[8]

Many of the most popular NLWs have been in existence for less than twenty years; nobody can claim a lifetime of experience in operating them. In fact, some opine that because NLWs are so new, so categorically different from the armaments that most police and military are familiar with, training on NLWs is even more important and more demanding than training with the mechanisms of deadly force. Practice with firearms is a fundamental part of basic and refresher training for most police and soldiers – there is no substitute for disciplined repetition – and nothing less should be required for those who might exercise NLWs.

We also must be especially alert to the danger that some candidate non-lethal technologies could be diverted for inappropriate uses. "Yankee ingenuity" on the battlefield occasionally leads to soldiers tinkering with their equipment in unforeseen ways. Sometimes these ad hoc adaptations provide an important practical augmentation, but sometimes they allow relatively benign capabilities to be distorted. Whether the trigger puller is a green eighteen-year-old soldier alone on a foreign battlefield or a seasoned cop on a familiar beat, thorough and frequently repeated training can provide at least part of the solution.

The U.S. military services, sensitive to these imperatives, have already devoted considerable resources to NLW training, including dedicated courses for deployed units, leaders, and NLW instructors. But it must be a perpetual commitment to ensure that the

---

[8] See Committee for an Assessment of Non-Lethal Weapons Science and Technology, Naval Studies Board, Division on Engineering and Physical Sciences, National Research Council, National Academies, An Assessment of Non-Lethal Weapons Science and Technology, 2003, pp. 87–93 (identifying multiple demands for training military on NLW effects, targeting, battle damage assessments, tactics, vulnerabilities, countermeasures, etc.).

fielded forces are adequately prepared for proper use of their new equipment.

10. DO NOT BE LULLED INTO OVERUSE OF NON-LETHAL WEAPONS

It is predictable that as the perceived *cost* of using force goes down, the *likelihood* of using force will go up. That is (at the management level), if national leaders believe we can apply non-lethal force effectively to resolve a hostage/barricade situation or to mitigate the risks of house-to-house combat, they will inevitably become somewhat more prone to commit the law enforcement or military resources to those tasks. Likewise (at the street level), if individual soldiers and police have increased confidence in the utility of their new NLW inventories, they surely, over time, will come to use those devices sooner and with less provocation.

Already we have witnessed something of that sort with electric shock weapons. Evidence suggests that when a police force becomes equipped with tasers for the first time, the number of incidents of use of deadly force plummets, as officers appropriately apply non-lethal electricity instead of deadly bullets. However, in those same communities, the overall total of all police uses of force inexorably rises, as officers come to engage the tasers quickly and perhaps pre-emptively, applying that level of intermediate power in many more situations where previously they would have found some way to handle the matter without resorting to violence at all.

It is difficult, but imperative, to avoid the type of lazy thinking that could lead to overreliance upon NLWs in inappropriate situations. We must not allow ourselves to be lulled into a false sense that weapons – even the relatively safe NLWs – could be wielded costlessly against foreign or domestic antagonists. Any confrontation must be approached with wisdom and restraint – there can never be a guaranty that NLWs will provide a safe, bloodless solution. The continuum of threats faced by police and military units – from a lone gunman all the way up to the paroxysms of Waco, Rwanda, Lima, Moscow, and Basra – are inherently dangerous, and the political process must never underestimate those risks or overestimate the ability of NLWs to dodge them.

Even the best arsenal of NLWs cannot promise cheap or easy solutions to the difficult and diverse crises that challenge police and military units. And injudicious invocation of NLWs – using the weapons inexpertly or in inapt situations – can certainly exacerbate a problem, leading to even higher levels of injuries, deaths, and destruction of property.

In sum, this book's analysis of five recent confrontations should not be read as an assertion that NLWs would have ensured a better outcome in Waco, Rwanda, Lima, Moscow, or Basra. It is entirely possible that none of those sorry circumstances could have been handled much better, even with an improved arsenal of deft NLW tools. Perhaps nothing (currently available or in prospect) could be sufficiently fast-acting, precise, safe, and powerful to be efficacious against such fanatic, suicidal opponents. Still, it is worth thinking about: these sorts of situations will continue to emerge around the world with some frequency, and if technology can provide any traction in helping to develop a strategy for handling them with greater success, we should explore all the options. As one of the U.S. government's experts commented upon reviewing the Waco debacle, "Hindsight is of little value except when it is used to provide new solutions to recurring problems."[9]

---

[9] Robert Cancro, letter to Deputy Attorney General Philip B. Heyman, August 30, 1993, reprinted in U.S. Department of Justice, Recommendations of Experts for Improvements in Federal Law Enforcement after Waco (1993), p. 6.

A variety of factors will, and should, push us increasingly into the realm of NLWs. The concept of NLWs is (or, at least, should be) both more effective and more humane, sparing civilians and operators alike some of the worst predations of conflict. Especially in an era when warfare impacts noncombatants with increasing frequency and brutality (in recent international and internal fighting of various sorts, upwards of 80 percent of the casualties have been civilians), NLWs should be welcome.[10]

At the same time, the impetus toward NLWs is not simply to be "nicer" to our opponents – the devices are intended primarily to provide better mechanisms for accomplishing the mission. They enable police and the military to behave more flexibly, more deftly, and more precisely, all of which translates into greater effective power. In too many current situations, our officials' hands are tied; in the absence of tools of finesse, they may be paralyzed by the chasm between lethal overreaction and feckless inaction.

Of course, the issue is not to choose between lethal and non-lethal force; the systems complement each other, and each can play a role in addressing these most vexing confrontations. The unique contribution of NLWs is to create more options, to provide police and military units with intermediate devices to assert power – systems that can deter, dissuade, disorient, disrupt, and disable, instead of jumping directly to destruction and death. They can help clarify obscure motivations and ambiguous situations, by halting or repelling the truly innocent and compelling the truly malicious to reveal their intentions. They enable authorities to separate the onlookers from the attackers, to afford each cadre the treatment it deserves.

---

[10] Margaret-Anne Coppernoll, The Nonlethal Weapons Debate, 52 *Naval War College Review* 112, spring 1998, p. 2.

In short, non-lethal weaponry will not replace traditional lethal force in these agonizing confrontations, but should supplement it, providing a cheaper, more flexible, more useable capability. There is, of course, always a danger in augmenting the power of governments, even those with apparently benign motivations, but in the case of selected revolutionary NLW technologies, that is a risk worth running.

Select Bibliography

Materials Relating to Chapter 4: The FBI and the Davidians at Waco in 1993

Activities of Federal Law Enforcement Agencies toward the Branch Davidians, Joint Hearings before the Subcommittee on Crime of the Committee on the Judiciary and the Subcommittee on National Security, International Affairs, and Criminal Justice of the Committee on Government Reform and Oversight, U.S. House of Representatives, 104th Congress, 1st session, Serial No. 72, July and August 1995.

Brad Bailey and Bob Darden, *Mad Man in Waco*, 1993.

Peter J. Boyer, The Children of Waco, *New Yorker,* May 15, 1995.

Committee on the Judiciary, in conjunction with the Committee on Government Reform and Oversight, U.S. House of Representatives, Materials Relating to the Investigation into the Activities of Federal Law Enforcement Agencies toward the Branch Davidians, 104th Congress, 2nd session, Serial No. 12, August 1996.

John C. Danforth, Final Report to the Deputy Attorney General Concerning the 1993 Confrontation at the Mt. Carmel Complex, Waco Texas, November 8, 2000 (and Interim Report, July 21, 2000).

Edward S. G. Dennis, Jr., U.S. Department of Justice, Evaluation of the Handling of the Branch Davidian Stand-Off in Waco, Texas, February 28 to April 19, 1993, redacted version, October 8, 1993.

Philip B. Heymann, Lessons of Waco: Proposed Changes in Federal Law Enforcement, October 8, 1993.

Dean M. Kelley, Waco: A Massacre and Its Aftermath, *First Things*, May 1995, p. 22.

Stephen Labaton and Sam Howe Verhovek, Missteps in Waco: A Raid Re-Examined, *New York Times*, March 28, 1993, p. A1.

James R. Lewis (ed.), *From the Ashes: Making Sense of Waco*, 1994.

Clifford L. Linedecker, *Massacre at Waco, Texas*, 1993.

Timothy Lynch, No Confidence: An Unofficial Account of the Waco Incident, Cato Institute Policy Analysis No. 395, April 9, 2001.

PBS Frontline, "Waco: The Inside Story," 2002, www.pbs.org/wgbh/pages/frontline/waco/view.

Dick J. Reavis, *The Ashes of Waco: An Investigation*, 1995.

Report of the Department of the Treasury on the Bureau of Alcohol, Tobacco, and Firearms Investigation of Vernon Wayne Howell, also known as David Koresh, September 1993.

U.S. Department of Justice, Recommendations of Experts for Improvements in Federal Law Enforcement after Waco, 1993.

U.S. Department of Justice, Report to the Deputy Attorney General on the Events at Waco, Texas, February 28 to April 19, 1993, redacted version, October 8, 1993.

Materials Relating to Chapter 5: The United Nations and the Rwandan Genocide in 1994

Howard Adelman and Astri Suhrke (eds.), *The Path of a Genocide: The Rwanda Crisis from Uganda to Zaire*, 1999.

Raymond Bonner, How Minority Tutsi Won the War, *New York Times*, September 6, 1994, p. A6.

Raymond Bonner, Nyakizu Journal: And the Church Refuge Became a Killing Field, *New York Times*, November 17, 1994, p. A4.

Raymond Bonner, Rebels in Rwanda Call a Cease-Fire: Exodus Continues, *New York Times*, July 19, 1994, p. A1.

Ingvar Carlsson, Han Sung-Joo, and Rufus M. Kupolati, United Nations, Report of the Independent Inquiry into the Actions of the United Nations during the 1994 Genocide in Rwanda, S/1999/1257, December 15, 1999.

Herman Cohen, Getting Rwanda Wrong, *Washington Post*, June 3, 1994, p. A23.

Alison Des Forges, Leave None to Tell the Story: Genocide in Rwanda, Human Rights Watch, 1999.

Scott R. Feil, Preventing Genocide: How the Early Use of Force Might Have Succeeded in Rwanda, Report to the Carnegie Commission on Preventing Deadly Conflict, April 1998.

Philip Gourevitch, *We Wish to Inform You That Tomorrow We Will Be Killed with Our Families: Stories from Rwanda,* 1998.

Adam Jones, Case Study: Genocide in Rwanda, 1994, Gendercide Watch, 2002.

Linda Kirschke, Broadcasting Genocide: Censorship, Propaganda, and State-Sponsored Violence in Rwanda, 1990–1994, published by Article 19, October 1996.

Alan J. Kuperman, *The Limits of Humanitarian Intervention: Genocide in Rwanda,* 2001.

Paul Lewis, Rebels in Rwanda Said to Slay 3 Bishops and 10 Other Clerics, *New York Times,* June 10, 1994, p. A1.

Paul Lewis, Vatican Asks U.N. for "Safe Area" in Rwanda, *New York Times,* June 1, 1994, p. A11.

Donatella Lorch, The Massacres in Rwanda: Hope Is Also a Victim, *New York Times,* April 21, 1994, p. A3.

Donatella Lorch, U.N. in Rwanda Says It Is Powerless to Halt the Violence, *New York Times,* April 15, 1994, p. A3.

Jennifer Parmelee, Americans Are Out of Rwanda: Rebel Army Advances on Bloodied Capital, *Washington Post,* April 11, 1994, p. A1.

Jennifer Parmelee, Fears Mounting for Rwandans: Aid Agencies Say Pullout of U.N. Peacekeepers Endangers Refugees, *Washington Post,* April 23, 1994, p. A14.

PBS Frontline, The Triumph of Evil: 100 Days of Slaughter: A Chronology of U.S./U.N. Actions, 1999.

Robert Pear, U.S. Envoy in Rwanda Decides on Overland Convoy to Evacuate Americans, *New York Times,* April 10, 1994, p. A6.

Julia Preston, 250,000 Flee Rwanda for Tanzania: Ethnic Warfare May Have Killed 200,000, U.N. Says, *Washington Post,* April 30, 1994, p. A1.

Julia Preston, U.N. Votes to Dispatch More Troops to Rwanda: Weapons Embargo Imposed on Both Sides, *Washington Post,* May 17, 1994, p. A12.

Gerard Prunier, *The Rwanda Crisis,* 1995.

Jonathan C. Randal, French Troops Race to Rescue of Tutsis: 1st Effort to Protect Rwandan Civilians, *Washington Post,* July 1, 1994, p. A27.

Jonathan C. Randal, Hutu Leaders Hanging on in Rwanda: Officials Reject Blame for Slaughter, *Washington Post,* July 8, 1994, p. A1.

Jonathan C. Randal, Rebels Take Chief Cities in Rwanda: French Forces Declare Protection Zones after Capital, Butare Fall, *Washington Post*, July 5, 1994, p. A1.

Jonathan C. Randal, Saved by French Troops, Rwandans Thank God: Tutsis Celebrate Mass under Guard, *Washington Post*, June 27, 1994, p. A1.

Keith B. Richburg, Rebel Victory Called Path to Ending Rwandan Slaughter, *Washington Post*, May 29, 1994, p. A48.

Keith B. Richburg, Trauma of Rwanda Helps Keep Burundi's Machetes Sheathed, *Washington Post*, June 10, 1994, p. A22.

Keith B. Richburg, U.N. General Sees No End in Rwanda: Canadian Predicts Continued "Horror Show" of More Massacres, *Washington Post*, June 11, 1994, p. A18.

Keith B. Richburg, Washington Begins to Act as Displaced Rwandans Wait, *Washington Post*, May 3, 1994, p. A14.

Keith B. Richburg, The World Ignored Genocide, Tutsis Say: As Rwanda Massacre Figure Grows, Slow Response Puzzles, Embitters Survivors, *Washington Post*, August 8, 1994, p. A1.

Christian P. Scherrer, *Genocide and Crisis in Central Africa: Conflict Roots, Mass Violence, and Regional War*, 2002.

William E. Schmidt, Troops Rampage in Rwanda: Dead Said to Include Premier, *New York Times*, April 8, 1994, p. A1.

Marlise Simons, French Troops Enter Rwanda in Aid Mission, *New York Times*, June 24, 1994, p. A1.

United Nations, *The United Nations and Rwanda 1993–1996*, Blue Book Series Volume X, 1996.

Alan Zarembo, Judgment Day, 294 *Harper's Magazine* No. 1763, April 1997, p. 68.

Materials Relating to Chapter 6: The Peruvians and Tupac Amaru in Lima in 1996–1997

Julissa Castellanos, ICE Case Studies: Tupac Amarau Uprising and the Environment, Case Number 23, June 1997.

Gabriel Escobar, Fujimori: Hostage Talks Limited but Asylum Possible, *Washington Post*, January 11, 1997, p. A1.

Gabriel Escobar, In Lima, the News Is Made by Overeager Reporters, *Washington Post*, January 9, 1997, p. A27.

Gabriel Escobar, Peru Buries Its 3 Fallen as Heros, *Washington Post*, April 25, 1997, p. A29.

Gabriel Escobar, Peru Raid Used Tunnels, Bugs: Commandos Waited Underground 3 Days to Launch Rescue, *Washington Post*, April 24, 1997, p. A1.

Gabriel Escobar, Peru's Hostage Gamble: The Drama and the Danger; A Network of Whispers on Residence's 2nd Floor, *Washington Post*, April 27, 1997, p. A1.

Gabriel Escobar, Peru's Leader Rejects Captors' Key Demand, *Washington Post*, December 20, 1996, p. A1.

Gabriel Escobar, Peru's Rulers Await "Real Negotiations": Signs Point to Standoff Following Massive yet Selective Release, *Washington Post*, December 24, 1996, p. A7.

Gabriel Escobar, Peruvian Guerrillas Hold Hundreds Hostage: Ambassadors among Those Detained, *Washington Post*, December 19, 1996, p. A1.

Gabriel Escobar, Peruvian Hostage Crisis Complicates American's Case, *Washington Post*, January 12, 1997, p. A23.

Gabriel Escobar, Rebels Classified Hostages by "Value": Freed Peruvian Describes Guerrillas' Methods, Demands, *Washington Post*, December 22, 1996, p. A1.

Gabriel Escobar, Red Cross Visits to Jailed Rebels Cut by Peru, *Washington Post*, December 27, 1996, p. A29.

Gabriel Escobar, Scenarios for Freeing Hostages Omit Emptying of Peru's Jails, *Washington Post*, January 26, 1997, p. A25.

Douglas Farah, Peru's Hostage Gamble: The Drama and the Danger; Elite Unit Spent Months Preparing Perfect Assault, *Washington Post*, April 27, 1997, p. A1.

Tori Hammond, In the Spotlight: Tupac Amaru Revolutionary Movement (MRTA), Center for Defense Information, November 18, 2003.

Peter Hillmore, Special Report: Over? It Is Now, *Guardian* (London), April 27, 1997, p. 3.

Mary Powers, Hostages Freed in Peru: Rebels Die in Army Raid, *Washington Post*, April 23, 1997, p. A1.

Diana Jean Schemo, Pact for Peru Hostage Crisis Is Said to Be on the Table, *New York Times*, March 22, 1997, p. A3.

Diana Jean Schemo, Peru Guerrillas and Hostages Face the Press, *New York Times*, January 1, 1997, p. A1.

Diana Jean Schemo, Talks Resume between Peru and Guerrillas, *New York Times*, January 12, 1997, p. A1.

Howard Schneider and Pamela Constable, Peru's Leader Vows to Avoid Using Force to Rescue Hostages, *Washington Post*, February 2, 1997, p. A1.

Philip Shenon, In Peru, A Brilliant Rescue Shines No Light on Terror, *New York Times*, April 27, 1997, sec. 4, p. 3.

Philip Shenon, Rescue in Peru: Strategies; Raid Stuck to the Rules, with a Few Twists, *New York Times*, April 24, 1997, p. A13.

Calvin Sims, Lima Journal: 80,000 Uneasy People, All Prisoners of Peru Crisis, *New York Times*, January 9, 1997, p. A4.

Calvin Sims, Peru Officials Admit to Plan for Commando Raid on Embassy, *New York Times*, February 17, 1997, p. A3.

Calvin Sims, Siege in Peru: Security: Peru Shrugged Off Warnings of Rebel Attack, Experts Say, *New York Times*, December 20, 1996, p. A1.

Geoff Stead, Glory and the Freedom Raiders, *Daily Telegraph* (Sydney, Australia), April 26, 1997, p. 32.

Special Operations.Com, Japanese Ambassador's Residence, Lima Peru, 1997.

Special Operations.Com, Peru's Special Forces, Operation Chavin de Huantar, 1997.

Materials Relating to Chapter 7: The Russians and the Chechens in Moscow in 2002

Brandt Ahrens, Note, Chechnya and the Right of Self-Determination, 42 *Columbia Journal of Transnational Law* 575, 2004.

Lawrence K. Altman, The Doctor's World: Moscow Toll Revives Concerns over Chemical Attacks, *New York Times*, November 5, 2002, p. F5.

Peter Baker, 50 Militants, 90 Hostages Dead after Moscow Siege, Gas Used to Subdue Chechens: Fate of Americans Unknown, *Washington Post*, October 27, 2002, p. A1.

Peter Baker, For Putin, A Little War That Won't End, *Washington Post*, October 26, 2002, p. A23.

Peter Baker and Susan B. Glasser, Putin Takes Hard Line on Terror, Stays Silent on Use of Deadly Gas, *Washington Post*, October 29, 2002, p. A11.

Peter Baker and Susan B. Glasser, Rebels Hold Hundreds Hostage in Moscow, Chechen Gunmen Take over Theater, *Washington Post*, October 24, 2002, p. A1.

Peter Baker and Susan B. Glasser, U.S. Ambassador Critical of Russia in Hostage Crisis: Gas Secrecy May Have Cost Lives, He Says, *Washington Post*, October 30, 2002, p. A14.

BBC News, Gas "Killed Moscow Hostages," October 27, 2002.

BBC News, The Moscow Theatre Siege, Transcript, January 15, 2004.

BBC News, Q&A: The Chechen Conflict, October 29, 2002.

William J. Broad, The World: Oh, What a Lovely War. If No One Dies, *New York Times*, November 3, 2002, sec. 4, p. 3.

David Brown and Peter Baker, Moscow Gas Likely a Potent Narcotic: Drug Normally Used to Subdue Big Game, *Washington Post*, November 9, 2002, p. A12.

Christian Caryl, Death in Moscow: The Aftermath, 49 *New York Review of Books* No. 20, December 19, 2002, p. 58.

David Chazan, BBC News, Chechen Rebel Divisions, October 26, 2002.

Carlotta Gall and Thomas de Waal, *Chechnya: Calamity in the Caucasus*, 1998.

Susan B. Glasser, Rescue Ended Days of Horror and Uncertainty, *Washington Post*, October 27, 2002, p. A1.

Susan B. Glasser, Russian Crisis Brings War Home, *Washington Post*, November 3, 2002, p. A1.

Susan B. Glasser and Peter Baker, Chechen Rebels Issue Threat: Officials Say Guerrillas Set to Release Foreigners, *Washington Post*, October 25, 2002, p. A1.

Susan B. Glasser and Peter Baker, Gas in Raid Killed 115 Hostages: Only 2 Slain by Rebels; More than 600 Remain Hospitalized in Moscow, *Washington Post*, October 28, 2002, p. A1.

Susan B. Glasser and Peter Baker, Russia Seizes Theater from Militants in Bloody Battle: Troops Kill Chechen Leader; Some Captives Dead, Wounded, *Washington Post*, October 26, 2002, p. A1.

Susan B. Glasser and Peter Baker, Russia Seizes Theater from Rebels: Troops Kill Chechen Leader in Bloody Battle; Some Hostages Reported Dead, *Washington Post*, October 27, 2002, p. A1.

Guy Gugliotta, U.S. Finds Hurdles in Search for Nonlethal Gas, *Washington Post*, November 1, 2002, p. A30.

Sharon LaFraniere, Setback Seen for Rebel Cause: Theater Takeover Is Predicted to Prolong War in Chechnya, *Washington Post*, October 28, 2002, p. A1.

Judith Miller and William J. Broad, Hostage Drama in Moscow: The Toxic Agent; U.S. Suspects Opiate in Gas in Russia Raid, *New York Times*, October 29, 2002, p. A1.

Monterey Institute of International Studies, Chemical and Biological Weapons Nonproliferation Program, The Moscow Theater Hostage Crisis: Incapacitants and Chemical Warfare, November 4, 2002.

Moscow Hostage Crisis: Criticism Mounts with Death Toll, *Center for Defense Information Russia Weekly* No. 229, October 30, 2002.

Steven Lee Myers, Hostage Drama in Moscow: Russia Responds; Putin Vows Hunt for Terror Cells around the World, *New York Times*, October 29, 2002, p. A1.

Steven Lee Myers, Hostage Drama in Moscow: The Toxic Agent; Official Silence on Gas Raises Vexing Questions, *New York Times*, October 28, 2002, p. A10.

Steven Lee Myers, Sabrina Tavernise, and Michael Wines, The Aftermath in Moscow: The Chronology; From Anxiety, Fear and Hope, the Deadly Rescue in Moscow, *New York Times*, November 1, 2002, p. A1.

Olga Oliker, *Russia's Chechen Wars 1994–2000: Lessons from Urban Combat,* 2001.

David Ruppe, CWC: Experts Differ on Whether Russian Hostage Rescue Violated Treaty, Global Security Newswire, October 30, 2002.

Serge Schmemann, The Chechens' Holy War: How Global Is It? *New York Times*, October 27, 2002, sec. 4, p. 3.

Timothy L. Thomas, The Battle of Grozny: Deadly Classroom for Urban Combat, *Parameters*, summer 1999, p. 87.

Dmitri V. Trenin, The Forgotten War: Chechnya and Russia's Future, Carnegie Endowment for International Peace, Policy Brief 28, November 2003.

Dmitri V. Trenin and Aleksei V. Malashenko with Anatol Lieven, *Russia's Restless Frontier: The Chechnya Factor in Post-Soviet Russia,* 2004.

U.S. Department of State, Chechen Terrorist Organizations: Statement of the Case, February 28, 2003.

Bob Van Damme, Moscow Theater Siege: A Deadly Gamble That Nearly Paid Off, 269 *Pharmaceutical Journal* 7224, November 16, 2002, p. 723.

Nick Paton Walsh, Families Claim Death Toll from Gas in Moscow Siege Kept Secret, *Guardian* (London), October 18, 2003.

Paul Wax, Charles E. Becker, and Steven C. Curry, Unexpected "Gas" Casualties in Moscow: A Medical Toxicology Perspective, 41 *Annals of Emergency Medicine* No. 5, May 2003, p. 700.

Michael Wines, The Aftermath in Moscow: Post-Mortem in Moscow; Russia Names Drug in Raid, Defending Use, *New York Times*, October 31, 2002, p. A1.

Michael Wines, Chechens Seize Moscow Theater, Taking as Many as 600 Hostages, *New York Times*, October 24, 2002, p. A1.

Michael Wines, Hostage Drama in Moscow: The Aftermath; Hostage Toll in Russia over 100; Nearly All Deaths Linked to Gas, *New York Times*, October 28, 2002, p. A1.

Michael Wines, Hostage Drama in Moscow: The Moscow Front; Chechens Kill Hostages in Siege at Russian Hall, *New York Times*, October 25, 2002, p. A1.

Michael Wines, Hostage Drama in Moscow: The Raid; At Least 67 Captives and 50 Chechens Die in Siege, *New York Times*, October 27, 2002, sec. 1, p. 1.

Michael Wines and Sabrina Tavernise, Russia Recaptures Theater after Chechen Rebel Group Begins to Execute Hostages, *New York Times*, October 26, 2002, p. A1.

Materials Relating to Chapter 8: The British and the Iraqis in Basra in 2003.

John M. Broder with Eric Schmitt, A Nation at War: The Plan; U.S. Attacks on Holdouts Dealt Iraqis Final Blow, *New York Times*, April 13, 2003, p. B1.

Oliver Burkeman, War in the Gulf: Basra: Battle for City Leads to "Massacre of Children" Claim: Allies Silent on Claim of Dozens Killed by Bombing, *Guardian* (London), March 24, 2003, p. 4.

Rajiv Chandrasekaran and Peter Baker, Troops Advance Halfway to Baghdad: Others Close in on Second-Largest City, *Washington Post*, March 23, 2003, p. A1.

James Dao, A Nation at War: Basra; Allied Air and Ground Units Try to Weaken Baath Party's Grip, *New York Times*, March 30, 2003, p. B6.

Dexter Filkins, A Nation at War: Southern Front; Eyes on Capital, U.S. Troops Flow Past the South, *New York Times*, March 24, 2003, p. B1.

Susan B. Glasser, Scars Document Torture by Hussein Regime, *Washington Post*, April 19, 2003, p. A1.

Susan B. Glasser and Richard Leiby, British See Uprising by Civilians in Basra, *Washington Post*, March 26, 2003, p. A1.

Michael R. Gordon, A Nation at War: Military Analysis; Basra Offers a Lesson on Taking Baghdad, *New York Times*, April 7, 2003, p. B1.

Michael R. Gordon, A Nation at War: The Strategy; U.S. Shifting Focus of Land Campaign to Fight in South, *New York Times*, March 26, 2003, p. A1.

Victor Mallet, Mark Nicholson, and Mark Odell, Attack on Basra Begins with Land and Sea Assault, *Financial Times* (London), March 21, 2003, p. 4.

Richard Norton-Taylor and Rory McCarthy, War in the Gulf: British Plan to Take Basra by Force: Commanders Consider Whether to Move into City to Take Advantage of Reported Uprising, *Guardian* (London), March 26, 2003, p. 4.

Jane Perlez with Marc Santora, A Nation at War: Aid Shipment, *New York Times*, March 29, 2003, p. B1.

Keith B. Richburg, Basra Defenders Burrow Into Residential Areas, *Washington Post*, March 24, 2003, p. A1.

Keith B. Richburg, British Forces Confronted by Guerrilla Tactics, *Washington Post*, March 25, 2003, p. A1.

Keith B. Richburg, British Forces Enter Basra as Residents Loot City, *Washington Post*, April 7, 2003, p. A1.

Keith B. Richburg, British Troops' Dual Role: Soldiers and Relief Workers; Near Basra, Forces Hand Out Food, Water as Fighting Continues, *Washington Post*, April 4, 2003, p. A29.

Keith B. Richburg, British Use Raids to Wear Down Iraqi Fighters, *Washington Post*, April 3, 2003, p. A25.

Keith B. Richburg, In Basra, Growing Resentment, Little Aid: Casualties Stoke Hostility over British Presence, *Washington Post*, April 9, 2003, p. A23.

Keith B. Richburg, In Pursuit of Answers, and Loot, in Basra, *Washington Post*, April 8, 2003, p. A1.

Keith B. Richburg, Lawlessness Spreads in Villages: As Bandits Rove, Allied Forces Are Blamed for Not Enforcing Order, *Washington Post*, March 29, 2003, p. A1.

Keith B. Richburg, Move on Basra Met by Strong Iraqi Resistance, *Washington Post*, March 23, 2003, p. A19.

Keith B. Richburg, People in Basra Contest Official View of Siege, *Washington Post*, April 15, 2003, p. A13.

Keith B. Richburg, Standoff at Basra Hints at Tough Time in Baghdad, *Washington Post*, March 30, 2003, p. A22.

Keith B. Richburg and Susan B. Glasser, Iraqi Tanks Try to Break Out of Basra: British Troops Bombard City, *Washington Post*, March 27, 2003, p. A23.

Marc Santora, A Nation at War: In the Field, Basra; British Soldiers' Long Battle for a Southern City's Trust Requires Bullets and Handshakes, *New York Times*, April 5, 2003, p. B3.

Marc Santora, A Nation at War: In the Field, New Leaders; In Basra, There's Wariness about the Same Old Faces, *New York Times*, April 10, 2003, p. B1.

Marc Santora and Craig S. Smith, A Nation at War: In the Field British Forces; Tension at Checkpoint, Fear Crossing Bridge, *New York Times*, March 31, 2003, p. A1.

Craig S. Smith, A Nation at War: In the Field, Basra; British Assault Captures Half of City in South, *New York Times*, April 7, 2003, p. A1.

Craig S. Smith, A Nation at War: Southern Iraq; Amid Ruins of Baath Party's Headquarters, a Town's Pervasive Sense of Fear Remains, *New York Times*, April 6, 2003, p. B10.

Craig S. Smith, A Nation at War: The South; Basra's Defenders Are Said to Be Desperate and Fearful, *New York Times*, April 4, 2003, p. B8.

Patrick E. Tyler, A Nation at War: The Attack; Airstrikes Continue as Allies Consider Timing of a Thrust, *New York Times*, March 29, 2003, p. A1.

Patrick E. Tyler, A Nation at War: The Attack; Allies outside Biggest Southern City, *New York Times*, March 23, 2003, p. A1.

Patrick E. Tyler, A Nation at War: The Attack; U.S. Bombs Ravage Targets in Baghdad; Waves of Troops Sweeping South Iraq, *New York Times*, March 22, 2003, p. A1.

Patrick E. Tyler, A Nation at War: The Attack, Taxi Suicide Blast Kills 4 Americans in New Iraq Tactic, *New York Times*, March 30, 2003, p. A1

Patrick E. Tyler with Steven Lee Myers, A Nation at War: Combat; Allies Strike in Baghdad and Press into Basra, *New York Times*, April 7, 2003, p. A1.

Nicholas Wade and Eric Schmitt, U.S. Use of Tear Gas Could Violate Treaty, Critics Say, *New York Times*, April 5, 2003, p. B13.

Other Materials

Michael Avery, David Rudovsky and Karen M. Blum, *Police Misconduct: Law and Litigation,* 3rd ed., 2003.

Materials Relating Generally to Non-Lethal Weapons

Eric Adams, Shoot to Not Kill, 262 *Popular Science* No. 5, May 2003, p. 88.
Steven Aftergood, The Soft-Kill Fallacy, and Barbara Rosenberg, Nonlethal Weapons May Violate Treaties, *Bulletin of the Atomic Scientists*, September/October 1994, p. 40.
John B. Alexander, Antimateriel Technology, 69 *Military Review* No. 10, October 1989, p. 29.
John B. Alexander, *Future War: Non-Lethal Weapons in 21st Century Warfare,* 1999.
John B. Alexander, Nonlethal Weapons: When Deadly Force Is Not Enough, 33 *The Futurist* No. 8, October 1999, p. 34.
John B. Alexander, Optional Lethality: Evolving Attitudes toward Non-lethal Weaponry, 23 *Harvard International Review* No. 2, July 1, 2001.
John B. Alexander, An Overview of the Future of Non-Lethal Weapons, 17 *Medicine, Conflict and Survival* No. 3, July–September 2001, p. 175.
John B. Alexander and Charles "Sid" Heal, Non-Lethal and Hyper-Lethal Weaponry, 13 *Small Wars and Insurgencies*, summer 2002, p. 121.
Lexi Alexander and Julia L. Klare, The Role of Non-Lethal Technologies in Operations Other than War, Institute for Defense Analyses, Alexandria, VA, IDA-D-1868, June 1996.
Jürgen Altmann, Acoustic Weapons: A Prospective Assessment: Sources, Propagation and Effects of Strong Sound, Occasional Paper No. 22, Cornell University Peace Studies Program, 1999.
Jürgen Altmann, Non-Lethal Weapons Technologies: The Case for Independent Scientific Analysis, 17 *Medicine, Conflict and Survival* No. 3, July–September 2001, p. 234.
American Civil Liberties Union of Southern California, Pepper Spray: A Magic Bullet under Scrutiny, fall 1993.

Amnesty International, Arming the Torturers: Electric Shock Torture and the Spread of Stun Technology, March 1997.

Amnesty International, United States of America: Excessive and Lethal Force? Amnesty International's Concerns about Deaths and Ill-Treatment Involving Police Use of Tasers, November 30, 2004.

Rick Atkinson, Lean, Not-So-Mean Marines Set for Somalia, *Washington Post*, February 25, 1995, p. A22.

Bengt Anderberg, Ove E. Bring, and Myron L. Wolbarsht, Blinding Laser Weapons and International Humanitarian Law, 29 *Journal of Peace Research* No. 3, August 1992, p. 287.

Alex Berenson, As Police Use of Tasers Soars, Questions over Safety Emerge, *New York Times*, July 18, 2004, p. A1.

Elliot Stanton Berke, The Chechnya Inquiry: Constitutional Commitment or Abandonment? 10 *Emory International Law Review* 879, 1996.

Anthony Bleetman and Richard Steyn, *The Advanced Taser: A Medical Review*, April 27, 2003.

British Columbia Police Commission, Recommendations of the Committee on the Use of Less than Lethal Force by Police Officers in British Columbia, July 1990.

Robert J. Bunker, Nonlethal Weapons: Terms and References, INSS Occasional Paper 15, USAF Institute for National Security Studies, December 1996.

Colin Burrows, Operationalizing Non-Lethality: A Northern Ireland Perspective, 17 *Medicine, Conflict and Survival* No. 3, July–September 2001, p. 260.

E. E. Casagrande, Non-Lethal Weapons: Implications for the RAAF, Royal Australian Air Force Air Power Studies Centre, Fairbairn, Australia, Paper No. 38, November 1995.

Commission for the Protection of Human Life in Armed Conflict and Commission of History of Military Law, Non-Lethal Weapons and the Law of Armed Conflict, Report of a Seminar at Mannheim, October 1997, Military Law and the Law of War Review, 1998, p. 303.

Committee for an Assessment of Non-Lethal Weapons Science and Technology, Naval Studies Board, Division on Engineering and Physical Sciences, National Research Council, National Academies, *An Assessment of Non-Lethal Weapons Science and Technology*, 2003.

Joseph W. Cook III, David P. Fiely, and Maura T. McGowan, Nonlethal Weapons: Technologies, Legalities, and Potential Policies, *Airpower Journal*, special edition, 1995.

Margaret-Anne Coppernoll, The Nonlethal Weapons Debate, 52 *Naval War College Review* 112, spring 1998.

Council on Foreign Relations, Independent Task Force, Malcolm Wiener, chair, Non-Lethal Technologies: Military Options and Implications, 1995.

Council on Foreign Relations, Independent Task Force Report: Nonlethal Technologies: Progress and Prospects, Richard Garwin, chair, 1999.

Council on Foreign Relations, Nonlethal Weapons and Capabilities, Report of an Independent Task Force, Graham Allison and Paul X. Kelley, co-chairs, Richard L. Garwin, project director, 2004.

Robin M. Coupland, "Calmatives" and "Incapacitants": Questions for International Humanitarian Law Brought by New Means and Methods of Warfare with New Effects? 19th Workshop of the Pugwash Study Group on the Implementation of the Chemical and Biological Weapons Conventions, April 26–7, 2003.

Robin M. Coupland and David Meddings, Mortality Associated with Use of Weapons in Armed Conflicts, Wartime Atrocities, and Civilian Mass Shootings: Literature Review, 319 *British Medical Journal* 407, August 14, 1999.

Anne-Marie Cusac, The Trouble with Tasers, *Progressive*, April 2005, p. 22.

Malcolm R. Dando, The Danger to the Chemical Weapons Convention from Incapacitating Chemicals, Strengthening the Chemical Weapons Convention, First CWC Review Conference Paper No. 4, March 2003.

Malcolm Dando, *A New Form of Warfare: The Rise of Non-Lethal Weapons*, 1996.

Malcolm Dando, Non-Lethal Weapons, in *Brassey's Defence Yearbook* 1996, ch. 22, p. 393.

Malcolm Dando (ed.), Non-Lethal Weapons: Technological and Operational Prospects, Jane's online special report, November 2000.

Bruce L. Danto, Medical Problems and Criteria Regarding Use of Tear Gas by Police, 8 *American Journal of Forensic Medicine and Pathology* No. 4, 1987, p. 317.

Isabelle Daoust, Robin Coupland, and Rikke Ishoey, New Wars, New Weapons? The Obligation of States to Assess the Legality of Means and

Methods of Warfare, 84 *International Review of the Red Cross* No. 846, June 2002, p. 345.

Neil Davison and Nick Lewer, Research Report Number 4, Centre for Conflict Resolution, Non-Lethal Weapons Research Project at Bradford University (UK), December 2003.

Neil Davison and Nick Lewer, Research Report Number 5, Centre for Conflict Resolution, Non-Lethal Weapons Research Project at Bradford University (UK), May 2004.

Neil Davison and Nick Lewer, Research Report Number 6, Centre for Conflict Resolution, Non-Lethal Weapons Research Project at Bradford University (UK), October 2004.

Neil Davidson and Nick Lewer, Research Report Number 7, Centre for Conflict Resolution, Non-Lethal Weapons Research Project at Bradford University (UK), May 2005.

Department of Defense Directive 3000.3, Policy for Non-Lethal Weapons, July 9, 1996.

Louise Doswald-Beck, Implementation of International Humanitarian Law in Future Wars, 52 *Naval War College Review* No. 1, winter 1999, p. 24.

James C. Duncan, A Primer on the Employment of Non-Lethal Weapons, 45 *Naval Law Review*, 1998, p. 1.

James C. Duncan, Where and How Should Non-Lethal Weapons Be Employed?, 6 *Journal of Counterterrorism & Security* No. 2, winter 1999.

Jonathan T. Dworken, Rules of Engagement, Lessons from Restore Hope, 74 *Military Review* No. 9, September 1994, p. 26.

Steven M. Edwards, John Granfield, and Jamie Onnen, Evaluation of Pepper Spray, National Institute of Justice, Research in Brief, February 1997.

Paul R. Evancoe, Non-Lethal Technologies Enhance Warrior's Punch, 78 *National Defense* No. 493, December 1993, p. 26.

Tobias Feakin, Research Report Number 3, Centre for Conflict Resolution, Non-Lethal Weapons Research Project at Bradford University (UK), August 2001.

Johannes Feierlein, Scientific and Technological Standards and Trends for NLW, 38 *Military Law and Law of War Review*, 1999, p. 397.

David P. Fidler, The International Legal Implications of "Non-Lethal" Weapons, 21 *Michigan Journal of International Law* 51, fall 1999.

David Fidler, Law Enforcement under the Chemical Weapons Convention: Interpretation of Article II.9(d) of the Chemical Weapons Convention in

Regard to the Use of Toxic Chemicals for Law Enforcement Purposes, memorandum to FAS Working Group, April 24, 2003, presented to the Open Forum on Challenges to the Chemical Weapons Ban, The Hague, May 1, 2002.

David P. Fidler, "Non-Lethal" Weapons and International Law: Three Perspectives on the Future, 17 *Medicine, Conflict and Survival* No. 3, July–September 2001, p. 194.

Mark Fischetti, Less-than-Lethal Weapons, 98 *Technology Review* No. 1, January 1995, p. 14.

Sydney J. Freedberg, Jr., Killing Me Softly, *National Journal*, May 11, 2002, p. 1382.

David A. Fulghum, Secret Carbon-Fiber Warheads Blinded Iraqi Air Defenses, 136 *Aviation Week & Space Technology* No. 17, April 27, 1992, p. 18.

Paola Gaeta, The Armed Conflict in Chechnya before the Russian Constitutional Court, 7 *European Journal of International Law* No. 4, 1996, p. 563.

Scott R. Gourley, Less-than-Lethal Weapons, *Jane's Defence Weekly*, July 17, 1996, p. 19.

John Granfield, Jami Onnen, and Charles S. Petty, Pepper Spray and In-Custody Deaths, International Association of Chiefs of Police, Executive Brief, March 1994.

Ernest Harper, A Call for a Definition of Method of Warfare in Relation to the Chemical Weapons Convention, 48 *Naval Law Review*, 2001, p. 132.

Charles Heal, Nonlethal Technology and the Way We Think of Force, 81 *Marine Corps Gazette* No. 1, January 1997, p. 26.

Sid Heal, Crowds, Mobs and Nonlethal Weapons, 80 *Military Review* No. 2, March/April 2000, p. 45.

David Hemenway and Douglas Weil, Phasers on Stun: The Case for Less Lethal Weapons, 9 *Journal of Policy Analysis and Management* No. 1, winter 1990, p. 94.

Howard Hu, Jonathan Fine, Paul Epstein, Karl Kelsey, Preston Reynolds, and Bailus Walker, Tear Gas – Harassing Agent or Toxic Chemical Weapon? 262 *Journal of the American Medical Association* No. 5, August 4, 1989, p. 660.

H. Range Hutson, Deirdre Anglin, Gilbert V. Pineda, Christopher J. Flynn, Marie A. Russell, and James J. McKeith, Law Enforcement K9 Dog Bites:

Injuries, Complications, and Trends, 29 *Annals of Emergency Medicine* No. 5, May 1997, p. 637.

Danielle L. Infeld, Precision-Guided Munitions Demonstrated Their Pinpoint Accuracy in Desert Storm: But Is a Country Obligated to Use Precision Technology to Minimize Collateral Civilian Injury and Damage? 26 *George Washington Journal of International Law and Economics* 1992, p. 109.

David Isenberg, US Chemical "Non-Lethal" Weapons in Iraq: A Violation of the Chemical Weapons Convention? BASIC Papers, Occasional Papers on International Security Policy No. 44, March 2003.

Joint Non-Lethal Weapons Directorate, Joint Concept for Non-Lethal Weapons, January 5, 1998.

Joint Non-Lethal Weapons Program, master plan, June 2000.

Joint Non-Lethal Weapons Program, Non-Lethal Weapons, Joint Mission Area Analysis/ Joint Mission Need Analysis, December 2000.

Jorma Jussila, Future Police Operations and Non-Lethal Weapons, 17 *Medicine, Conflict and Survival* No. 3, July–September 2001, p. 248.

John M. Kenny, Sid Heal, and Mike Grossman, The Attribute-Based Evaluation (ABE) of Less-than-Lethal, Extended-Range, Impact Munitions, Pennsylvania State University, February 15, 2001.

John M. Kenny, Clark McPhail, Peter Waddington, Sid Heal, Steve Ijames, Donald N. Farrer, Jim Taylor, and Dick Odenthal, Crowd Behavior, Crowd Control, and the Use of Non-Lethal Weapons, Pennsylvania State University, Institute for Non-Lethal Defense Technologies, January 1, 2001.

Jonathan W. Klaaren and Ronald S. Mitchell, Nonlethal Technology and Airpower, *Airpower Journal*, special edition, 1995.

Lynn Klotz, Martin Furmanski, and Mark Wheelis, Beware the Siren's Song: Why "Non-Lethal" Incapacitating Chemical Agents Are Lethal, March 2003.

Richard Kokoski, Non-Lethal Weapons: A Case Study of New Technology Developments, in *SIPRI Yearbook 1994*, ch. 11, p. 367.

Eric M. Koscove, The Taser Weapon: A New Emergency Medicine Problem, 14 *Annals of Emergency Medicine* No. 12, December 1985, p. 1205.

F. Kruger-Sprengel, Innovative Legal Effects of Non-Lethal Weapons (NLW) for Political and Military Strategy and for Humanitarian Intervention, 38 *Military Law and Law of War Review*, 1999, p. 383.

Friedhelm Kruger-Sprengel, Non-Lethal Weapons: A Humanitarian Perspective in Modern Conflict, 42 *Military Law and the Law of War Review* Nos. 3–4, 2003, p. 359.

Joan M. Lakoski, W. Bosseau Murray, and John M. Kenny, The Advantages and Limitations of Calmatives for Use as a Non-Lethal Technique, Applied Research Laboratory, College of Medicine, Pennsylvania State University, October 3, 2000.

Timothy J. Lamb, Emerging Nonlethal Weapons Technology and Strategic Policy Implications for 21st Century Warfare, thesis, U.S. Army War College, Carlisle Barracks, Penn., 1998.

Erik Larson, Nonlethal Weapons: Freeze, or I'll Fire My Sticky-Goo Gun: Law Enforcement Researchers Develop Benign Devices, but They Have Drawbacks, *Wall Street Journal*, August 2, 1994, p. A1.

"Law Enforcement" and the CWC (editorial), 58 *Chemical and Biological Weapons Conventions Bulletin*, December 2002, p. 1.

Nick Lewer (ed.), *The Future of Non-Lethal Weapons: Technologies, Operations, Ethics, and Law*, 2002.

Nick Lewer, Introduction to Non-Lethal Weapons, Research Report Number 1, Centre for Conflict Resolution, Non-Lethal Weapons Research Project at Bradford University (UK), November 1997.

Nick Lewer, Objections to Weapons of Less Destruction, 33 *Futurist* No. 8, October 1999, p. 39.

Nick Lewer, Research Report Number 2, Centre for Conflict Resolution, Non-Lethal Weapons Research Project at Bradford University (UK), June 1998.

Nick Lewer and Neil Davison, Non-Lethal Technologies: An Overview, *Disarmament Forum* No. 1, 2005, p. 36.

Nick Lewer and Tobias Feakin, Perspectives and Implications for the Proliferation of Non-Lethal Weapons in the Context of Contemporary Conflict, Security Interests and Arms Control, 17 *Medicine, Conflict and Survival* No. 3, July–September 2001, p. 272.

Nick Lewer, Tobias Feakin, and Malcolm Dando, The Future of Non-Lethal Weapons, 17 *Medicine, Conflict and Survival* No. 3, July–September 2001, p. 180.

Nick Lewer and Steven Schofield, *Non-Lethal Weapons: A Fatal Attraction? Military Strategies and Technologies for 21st Century Conflict*, 1997.

James B. Linder, A Case for Employing Nonlethal Weapons, 76 *Military Review* No. 5, September–October 1996, p. 25.

F. M. Lorenz, Law and Anarchy in Somalia, *Parameters*, winter 1993–4, p. 27.

Frederick M. Lorenz, "Less-Lethal" Force in Operation UNITED SHIELD, *Marine Corps Gazette*, September 1995, p. 68.

F. M. Lorenz, Nonlethal Force: The Slippery Slope to War? 27 *Parameters* No. 3, autumn 1996, p. 52.

Douglas C. Lovelace, Jr. and Steven Metz, Nonlethality and American Land Power: Strategic Context and Operational Concepts, U.S. Army War College, Strategic Studies Institute, June 15, 1998.

Richard C. Lumb and Paul C. Friday, Impact of Pepper Spray Availability on Police Officer Use-of-Force Decisions, 20 *Policing* No. 1, 1997, p. 136.

M. S. Meselson and J. P. Perry Robinson, "Non Lethal" Weapons and Implementation of the Chemical and Biological Weapons Conventions, paper for the 20th Pugwash Workshop Study Group on the Implementation of the CBW Conventions, November 8–9, 2003.

Stephen Mihm, The Quest for the Nonkiller App, *New York Times Magazine*, July 25, 2004, p. 38.

Neal Miller, Less-than-Lethal Force Weaponry: Law Enforcement and Correctional Agency Civil Law Liability for the Use of Excessive Force, 28 *Creighton Law Review* No. 3, April 1995, p. 733.

Eugene V. Morabito and William G. Doerner, Police Use of Less-than-lethal Force: Oleoresin Capsicum (OC) Spray, 20 *Policing* No. 4, 1997, p. 680.

David A. Morehouse, *Nonlethal Weapons: War without Death*, 1996.

Chris Morris, Janet Morris, and Thomas Baines, Weapons of Mass Protection: Nonlethality, Information Warfare, and Airpower in the Age of Chaos, *Airpower Journal*, spring 1995, p. 15.

Janet Morris, Enter Nonlethal Weaponry, 28 *IEEE Spectrum* No. 9, September 1991, p. 58.

David C. Morrison, Alternatives to Bashing, *National Journal*, June 6, 1992, p. 1358.

David Morrison, War without Death? *National Journal*, November 7, 1992, p. 2589.

National Institute of Justice, Office of Justice Programs, The Effectiveness and Safety of Pepper Spray, Research for Practice, April 2003.

NATO Policy on Non-Lethal Weapons, Press Statement, October 13, 1999.

Nonlethal Weapons Give Peacekeepers Flexibility, 137 *Aviation Week & Space Technology* No. 23, December 7, 1992, p. 50.

Paul G. O'Connor, Waging Wars with Nonlethal Weapons, in Karl P. Magyar (ed.), Challenge and Response: Anticipating US Military Security Concerns, Air University Press, Maxwell AFB, 1994, p. 333.

Omega Foundation, Baton Rounds: A Review of the Human Rights Implications of the Introduction and Use of the L21A1 Baton Round in Northern Ireland and Proposed Alternatives to the Baton Round, Northern Ireland Human Rights Commission, March 2003.

Omega Foundation (Manchester, UK), Crowd Control Technologies: An Appraisal of Technologies for Political Control, working document for the STOA Panel, European Parliament, PE 168.394/Fin.St., Luxembourg, June 2000.

Jami Onnen, Oleoresin Capsicum, report for International Association of Chiefs of Police, June 1993.

Gary J. Ordog, Jonathan Wasserberger, Theodore Schlater, and Subramaniam Balasubramanium, Electric Gun (Taser) Injuries, 16 Annals of Emergency Medicine No. 1, January 1987, p. 73.

W. Hays Parks, Air War and the Law of War, 32 Air Force Law Review No. 1, 1990.

Patten Report Recommendations 69 and 70 Relating to Public Order Equipment, A Research Programme into Alternative Policing Approaches towards the Management of Conflict, Third Report, December 2002.

Patten Report Recommendations 69 and 70 Relating to Public Order Equipment, A Research Programme into Alternative Policing Approaches towards the Management of Conflict, Fourth Report, January 2004.

Rupert Pengelley, Wanted: A Watch on Non-Lethal Weapons, Jane's International Defense Review, April 1, 1994.

Lois Pilant, Crime and War: An Analysis of Non-Lethal Technologies and Weapons Development, 65 Police Chief No. 6, June 1998, p. 55.

Lois Pilant, Less-than-Lethal Weapons: New Solutions for Law Enforcement, International Association of Chiefs of Police, Executive Brief, December 1993.

Gerrard Quille, The Revolution in Military Affairs Debate and Non-Lethal Weapons, 17 Medicine, Conflict and Survival No. 3, July–September 2001, p. 207.

Brian Rappert, A Framework for the Assessment of Non-Lethal Weapons, 20 Medicine, Conflict and Survival, 2004, p. 35.

Brian Rappert, Non-Lethal Weapons as Legitimizing Forces? Technology, Politics and the Management of Conflict, 2003.

Brian Rappert, Scenarios on the Future of Non-Lethal Weapons, 22 *Contemporary Security Policy* No. 1, April 2001, p. 57.

Brian Rappert and Steve Wright, A Flexible Response? Assessing Non-Lethal Weapons, 12 *Technology Analysis and Strategic Management* No. 4, 2000, p. 477.

Thomas E. Ricks, Nonlethal Arms: New Class of Weapons Could Incapacitate Foe yet Limit Casualties, *Wall Street Journal*, January 4, 1993, p. A1.

M. N. Robinson, C. G. Brooks, and G. D. Renshaw, Electric Shock Devices and Their Effects on the Human Body, 30 *Medicine, Science and Law* No. 4, 1990, p. 285.

Barbara Hatch Rosenberg, Riot Control Agents and the Chemical Weapons Convention, paper for the Open Forum on Challenges to the Chemical Weapons Ban, The Hague, May 1, 2003.

Linda Rothstein, The "Soft Kill" Solution, *Bulletin of the Atomic Scientists*, March–April 1994, p. 4.

Harvey M. Sapolsky, War without Killing, chapter 2 in Sam C. Sarkesian and John Mead Flanagin (eds.), *US Domestic and National Security Agendas: Into the 21st Century*, Contributions in Military Studies, No. 152, 1994.

Vincent Sautenet, Legal Issues Concerning Military Use of Non-Lethal Weapons, 7 *Murdoch University Electronic Journal of Law* No. 2, June 2000.

Eric Schmitt, Now, to the Shores of Somalia with Beanbag Guns and Goo, *New York Times*, February 15, 1995, p. A10.

Greg R. Schneider, Nonlethal Weapons: Considerations for Decision Makers, ACDIS Occasional Paper (University of Illinois, Program in Arms Control, Disarmament, and International Security), January 1997.

Security Planning Corporation, Nonlethal Weapons for Law Enforcement: Research Needs and Priorities, Report to the National Science Foundation, 1972.

Joseph Siniscalchi, Non-Lethal Technologies: Implications for Military Strategy, Center for Strategy and Technology, Air War College, Occasional Paper No. 3, March 1998.

Martin Stanton, Nonlethal Weapons: Can of Worms, 122 *US Naval Institute Proceedings* No. 11, November 1996, p. 58.

Martin N. Stanton, What Price Sticky Foam? 26 *Parameters* No. 3, autumn 1996, p. 3.

Sunshine Project, Non-Lethal Weapons Research in the United States: Genetically Engineered Anti-Material Weapons, *Backgrounder* No. 9, March 2002.

Sunshine Project, Non-Lethal Weapons Research in the US: Calmatives and Malodorants, *Backgrounder* No. 8, July 2001.

Sherri Sweetman, Report on the Attorney General's Conference on Less than Lethal Weapons, U.S. Department of Justice, National Institute of Justice, March 1987.

Charles Swett and Dan Goure, Non-Lethal Weapons Policy Study, Final Report, Center for Strategic and International Studies, Washington, D.C., February 5, 1999.

Alvin Toffler and Heidi Toffler, *War and Anti-War: Survival at the Dawn of the 21st Century,* 1993.

Amy Truesdell, The Ethics of Non-Lethal Weapons, Occasional Paper Number 24, Strategic and Combat Studies Institute, Staff College, Camberley (U.K.), 1996.

United Kingdom, Defence Scientific Advisory Council (DSAC) Sub-Committee on the Medical Implications of Less-lethal Weapons (DOMILL), Second DOMILL Statement on Medical Implications of the Use of the M26 Advanced Taser, DSTL/CBS/BTP/PAT-ACPO/MAN/REP/4/, July 27, 2004 (with annex of First DOMILL Statement, dated December 9, 2002).

United Kingdom, Defence Scientific Advisory Council (DSAC) Sub-Committee on the Medical Implications of Less Lethal Weapons (DOMILL), Statement on the Comparative Medical Implications of the Use of the X26 Taser and the M26 Advanced Taser, Dstl/BSC/BTP/DOC/803, March 7, 2005.

U.S. Joint Non-Lethal Weapons Program, Kosovo Incident Case Study: Use of Non-Lethal Weapons, April 4, 2000.

V. J. Wallace, Non-Lethal Weapons: R2IPE for Arms Control Measures? 1 *Defence Studies* No. 2, summer 2001, p. 83.

Mark Wheelis, "Nonlethal" Chemical Weapons: A Faustian Bargain, 19 *Issues in Science and Technology* No. 3, spring 2003, p. 74.

Mark Wheelis, Will the New Biology Lead to New Weapons? and The Danger of "Nonlethal" Weapons, 34 *Arms Control Today* No. 6, July/August 2004, p. 6.

Mark Wheelis and Malcolm Dando, Back to Bioweapons? 59 *Bulletin of the Atomic Scientists* No. 1, January/February 2003, p. 40.

Mark Wheelis and Malcolm Dando, New Technology and Future Developments in Biological Warfare, *Disarmament Forum* 4, 2000, p. 43.

Mark Wheelis and Malcolm Dando, On the Brink: Biodefence, Biotechnology and the Future of Weapons Control, 58 *Chemical and Biological Weapons Conventions Bulletin*, December 2002, p. 3.

J. P. Winthrop, Preliminary Legal Review of Proposed Chemical-Based Nonlethal Weapons, Department of the Navy, Office of the Judge Advocate General, International and Operational Law Division, National Security Law Branch, November 30, 1997.

Steve Wright, The New Technologies of Political Repression: A New Case for Arms Control? 17 *Philosophy and Social Action* Nos. 3–4, July–December 1991, p. 31.

Steve Wright, The Role of Sub-Lethal Weapons in Human Rights Abuse, 17 *Medicine, Conflict and Survival* No. 3, July–September 2001, p. 221.

Steve Wright, Omega Foundation, An Appraisal of the Technologies of Political Control, Luxembourg: European Parliament, Directorate General for Research, Directorate A, Division of Industry, Research and Energy, Scientific and Technological Options Assessment (STOA), PE 166 499, January 6, 1998.

Jean-Paul Yih, CS Gas Injury to the Eye, 311 *British Medical Journal* No. 7000, July 29, 1995, p. 276.

Index